ROBERT M. WEST

Christian Basics

66 Essential Truths
Explained and Applied

BARBOUR
PUBLISHING

Cover Design: Greg Jackson, Thinkpen Design

Published by Barbour Publishing, Inc., 1810 Barbour Drive, Uhrichsville, Ohio 44683, www.barbourbooks.com

Our mission is to inspire the world with the life-changing message of the Bible.

Member of the
Evangelical Christian
Publishers Association

Printed in the United States of America.

Contents

Introduction

In one sense, it's very easy to be a Christian. According to the apostle Paul, "If you declare with your mouth, 'Jesus is Lord,' and believe in your heart that God raised him from the dead, you will be saved" (Romans 10:9 NIV).

On the other hand, Christianity grows out of an old, very large book, hundreds of pages packed full of names and places, ideas and commands. To take the free and easy gift of salvation to the next level (a level that God desires for every believer), we need to grasp several important theological concepts. That's what this little book is about.

Now, don't let the word *theological* scare you away. It just indicates a study of God and the things of God—ideas such as the Trinity, worship, creation, sin, and redemption. All of those topics, and some five dozen others, will be addressed in *Christian Basics* to help you better understand God, His world, and your place in it.

In this little volume, you'll find brief entries on 66 vital aspects of the Christian faith. Each entry summarizes that particular point, giving you a clearer view of its meaning and importance. Every entry follows this outline:

- IN TEN WORDS OR LESS: A "nutshell" glance at the topic.

- DETAILS, PLEASE: A longer explanation, incorporating information from throughout God's Word.

- ADDITIONAL SCRIPTURES: A few other key verses supporting the point.

- WHAT OTHERS SAY: A memorable quotation from a pastor, theologian, or Christian author.

- SO WHAT? An inspirational or devotional thought as a personal takeaway.

The choice to become a Christian is the most important decision anyone can make. The choice to study and understand God's Word follows closely along, as you learn more about the loving God who created you, keeps you, and gives you eternal life through His Son, Jesus Christ.

Use this book to begin a journey of discovery that could truly change your life!

God

IN TEN WORDS OR LESS

God is the supreme Being who created and rules everything.

DETAILS, PLEASE

Who is God, and what is He like? He reveals Himself best in scripture and creation (Psalm 19). He said of Himself, "I am God, and there is no other; I am God, and there is none like Me" (Isaiah 46:9 NKJV). Genesis 1:1 indicates that the living God is the wise and powerful Creator who transcends His creation.

While He is infinite, God also wants a personal relationship with each one of us. So that we can better understand and enjoy Him, He revealed Himself in the person of the Lord Jesus Christ, who said, "He that hath seen me hath seen the Father" (John 14:9). When we know Jesus, we know God completely.

ADDITIONAL SCRIPTURES

- Do you not know? Have you not heard? The LORD is the everlasting God, the Creator of the ends of the earth. He will not grow tired or weary, and his understanding no one can fathom. (Isaiah 40:28 NIV)

- But you, O Lord, are a God merciful and gracious, slow to anger and abounding in steadfast love and faithfulness. (Psalm 86:15 ESV)

- He. . .is the blessed and only Potentate, the King of kings and Lord of lords, who alone has immortality, dwelling in unapproachable light, whom no man has seen or can see, to whom be honor and everlasting power. Amen. (1 Timothy 6:15–16 NKJV)

WHAT OTHERS SAY

Taking the total testimony of scripture. . .there is a harmonious presentation of the characteristics of God. *Robert P. Lightner*

SO WHAT?

Our infinite, transcendent Creator mercifully offers us a relationship with Him, through his Son, Jesus.

Jesus Christ

IN TEN WORDS OR LESS

Jesus is the incarnate God, Lord of heaven and earth.

DETAILS, PLEASE

Jesus' disciples gradually learned who He was. During one terrifying experience in their training, He calmed a storm on the Sea of Galilee. They asked each other, "Who can this be?" (Matthew 8:27 NKJV). Later Jesus asked them, "Who do *you* say that I am?" (Matthew 16:15 NKJV, emphasis added). Simon Peter answered correctly, "Thou art the Christ, the Son of the living God" (verse 16). Jesus then informed Peter that he was blessed because the heavenly Father had revealed this truth to him (verse 17).

The apostle John recorded seven different sign-miracles out of the many things that Jesus did to illustrate His divine authority over human tragedies. These were miracles with a message pointing to something greater. He explained his purpose for recording them: "These are written that ye might believe that Jesus is the Christ, the Son of God; and that believing ye might have life through his name" (John 20:31). Here is a list of those signs: (1) Jesus changed water into fine wine, revealing Himself as the powerful Creator of quality (2:1–11). (2) He healed a government official's son who was sixteen miles away, showing His authority over distance (4:46–54). (3) He healed a man paralyzed for thirty-eight years, exhibiting His control over time (5:1–15). (4) He fed the five thousand, revealing Himself as the Lord over quantity (6:5–14). (5) He walked on water during a storm, displaying His control over the dangerous forces of nature (6:16–21). (6) He healed a man born blind, demonstrating His sovereignty over misfortune; as "the light of the world," He granted physical sight (9:1–7) and spiritual sight (9:35–38). (7) He raised Lazarus from the grave, showing that He is "the resurrection and the life," who conquers death (11:1–45).

Just seeing Jesus' miraculous signs didn't guarantee that people would follow Him. At the end of Jesus' public ministry, John said, "Though he had done so many miracles before them, yet they believed not on him" (12:37). When the resurrected Jesus appeared to "doubting" Thomas, who demanded proof that Jesus had risen again, Jesus said to him, "Blessed are they that have not seen, and yet have believed" (20:29).

ADDITIONAL SCRIPTURES

- Behold the Lamb of God, which taketh away the sin of the world (John 1:29)

- But unto the Son he saith, Thy throne, O God, is for ever and ever. (Hebrews 1:8)

- For I delivered unto you first of all that which I also received, how that Christ died for our sins according to the scriptures; and that he was buried, and that he rose again the third day according to the scriptures. (1 Corinthians 15:3–4)

- Ye men of Galilee, why stand ye gazing up into heaven? this same Jesus, which is taken up from you into heaven, shall so come in like manner as ye have seen him go into heaven. (Acts 1:11)

WHAT OTHERS SAY

Although no other person is the object of more scriptural revelation, human pens falter when attempting to describe Him. *John F. Walvoord*

SO WHAT?

There is much to learn about Jesus. We must continually grow in grace and knowledge of our Lord and Savior.

Holy Spirit

IN TEN WORDS OR LESS

The Spirit is the third person of the triune Godhead.

DETAILS, PLEASE

Called "God" in Acts 5:3–4, the Holy Spirit is eternal (Hebrews 9:14) and created all things (Genesis 1:1–3 and Job 33:4). More than an impersonal force, He expresses emotion (Ephesians 4:30) and is identified by the personal pronouns "He" (John 15:26 NKJV) and "Himself" (Romans 8:16 NASB). The title "Holy Spirit" (Matthew 1:18 NASB) is synonymous with earlier English versions of "Holy Ghost." As God's gift (Acts 2:38), He gives spiritual life to all believers (John 3:3–8), who become temples of the Holy Spirit (1 Corinthians 6:19) having been baptized into Christ (1 Corinthians 12:13). He exhibits His presence by "the fruit of the Spirit" that He produces in believers' lives (Galatians 5:22–23), those who "walk by the Spirit" (verse 16 NASB).

ADDITIONAL SCRIPTURES

- Not by works of righteousness which we have done, but according to His mercy He saved us, through the washing of regeneration and renewing of the Holy Spirit. (Titus 3:5 NKJV)
- And I will pray the Father, and he shall give you another Comforter, that he may abide with you for ever; even the Spirit of truth; whom the world cannot receive, because it seeth him not, neither knoweth him: but ye know him; for he dwelleth with you, and shall be in you. (John 14:16–17)

WHAT OTHERS SAY

The Spirit-filled life is not a special, deluxe edition of Christianity. It is part and parcel of the total plan of God for His people. *A. W. Tozer*

SO WHAT?

God's Spirit is given to every believer to know Him and experience transformation by His power.

The Trinity

IN TEN WORDS OR LESS

Trinity describes the transcendent nature of the one triune God.

DETAILS, PLEASE

Although the term *Trinity* does not appear in the Bible, this mysterious concept throughout scripture describes the one true and living God who exists as three coequal and coeternal Persons. The term does not suggest that Christians worship a god who manifests Himself in three ways or that they worship three different gods, but it best describes the triune nature of the one true God. Christians are monotheistic, believing in one God, who declared in Deuteronomy 32:39 (NKJV), "Now see that I, even I, am He, and there is no God besides Me."

The early days of the Old Testament hint at a plurality in God's being. Over time, as God gave additional revelation about His nature in the New Testament, clarity was brought to this trinitarian concept. Although the thought of God being three in one may sound like a contradiction, the church developed its trinitarian belief not from pagan superstitions but from the following biblical truths:

First, throughout scripture all three divine Persons are called "God" (the Father, Galatians 1:1; the Son, Micah 5:2; the Spirit, Acts 5:3–4). Jesus received worship as God (John 20:28) and was criticized by His enemies for making Himself equal with God (John 5:18).

Second, all three Persons have the same divine attributes. For example, God is eternal (this is said of the Father, Psalm 90:2; the Son, John 8:58; and the Spirit, Hebrews 9:14).

Third, all three Persons do divine works that only God can do. Each was involved in creation (the Father, Genesis 1:1; the Son, Colossians 1:15–17; the Spirit, Genesis 1:2). Genesis 1:26–27 confirms the existence of the Trinity by the use of the plural pronouns "us" and "our," describing God's image: "Let *us* make man in *our* image" (emphasis added).

Fourth, Jesus' formula for the baptism ritual (Matthew 28:19) uses the one singular triune description of the Godhead.

Finally, all three Persons are acknowledged in the apostolic benediction in 2 Corinthians 13:14, which describes God's spiritual blessings.

No wonder King David offered praise for God's uniqueness in the Psalms: "Among the gods there is none like You, O Lord" (86:8 NKJV).

ADDITIONAL SCRIPTURES

- Hear, O Israel: The LORD our God is one LORD. (Deuteronomy 6:4)

- When He had been baptized, Jesus came up immediately from the water; and behold the heavens were opened to Him, and He saw the Spirit of God descending like a dove and alighting upon Him. And suddenly a voice came from heaven, saying, "This is My beloved Son, in whom I am well pleased." (Matthew 3:16–17 NKJV)

- "When the Helper comes, whom I will send to you from the Father, that is the Spirit of truth who proceeds the Father, He will testify about Me." (John 15:26 NASB)

- . . .elect according to the foreknowledge of God the Father, through sanctification of the Spirit, unto obedience and sprinkling of the blood of Jesus Christ. (1 Peter 1:2)

WHAT OTHERS SAY

The doctrine of the Trinity is basic to the Christian religion. It is no exaggeration to assert that the whole of Christianity stands or falls with it. *R. B. Kuiper*

SO WHAT?

Because God the Father, God the Son, and God the Holy Spirit are equal, each divine Person in the Godhead is worthy of our equal worship and devotion.

Worship

IN TEN WORDS OR LESS

Worship involves adoring God with reverent devotion and praise.

DETAILS, PLEASE

The apostle Paul discussed worship in his letter to the Romans, urging believers to offer their entire lives to God in heartfelt adoration and service. He said, "Therefore I urge you, brethren, by the mercies of God, to present your bodies a living and holy sacrifice, acceptable to God, which is your spiritual service of worship" (Romans 12:1 NASB). Based on God's saving work for us, we are to present ourselves to God. This personal sacrifice is to be "living and holy" in contrast to an offering of sacrificial animals killed on an altar. The following verses further explain that our presentation should involve separation from negative worldly influences and a transformation in our lifestyle accomplished by renewed biblical thinking.

ADDITIONAL SCRIPTURES

- "But an hour is coming, and now is, when the true worshipers will worship the Father in spirit and truth; for such people the Father seeks to be His worshipers. God is spirit, and those who worship Him must worship in spirit and truth." (John 4:23–24 NASB)

- For we are of the circumcision, which worship God in the spirit, and rejoice in Christ Jesus, and have no confidence in the flesh. (Philippians 3:3)

- O come, let us worship and bow down: let us kneel before the LORD our maker. (Psalm 95:6)

- Worship the LORD in the splendor of his holiness; tremble before him, all the earth. (Psalm 96:9 NIV)

WHAT OTHERS SAY

Worship is an inward feeling and outward action that reflects the worth of God. *John Piper*

SO WHAT?

Worship is much more than the music service at church—it includes our every thought and action.

Creation

IN TEN WORDS OR LESS

Creation is God's act of bringing the universe into existence.

DETAILS, PLEASE

The creation story in Genesis 1 and 2 begins with God: "In the beginning God created" (1:1). Colossians 1:15–17 adds to this by describing the exalted Creator, the Lord Jesus Christ. Verse 15 calls Him "the image of the invisible God," meaning that He's a perfect representation of what God the Father, whom we cannot see, is like. If you want to see God, look at Jesus who said, "He that hath seen me hath seen the Father" (John 14:9). In Colossians 1 Jesus is also called "the firstborn over all creation" (verse 15 NKJV), which describes His exalted position over everything.

Verse 16 explains that Christ is given this "firstborn" title because He created everything. This includes unseen things such as the wind, as well as heaven's invisible angelic beings (grouped into four categories called "thrones, or dominions, or principalities, or powers"). Jesus' creative activity also includes all visible things, from the vast universe of planets to the pinnacle of His creation, mankind, whom He made in His own image "male and female" (Genesis 1:27).

Colossians 1:16 ends by stating all things were created *by* Him (He is the architect and the builder), and everything was created *for* Him (for His enjoyment and glory). Just as, during Jesus' time of ministry, a firstborn son had more stature in a family, Christ is preeminent as Creator.

The apostle Paul's description of Jesus ends in verse 17 by saying, "He is before all things" (NASB). Jesus is the source of everything, who also sustains all of creation: "In Him all things hold together."

Many people today sound warnings about climate change destroying the world if there is no change in human behavior. But God reveals that our biggest problem isn't ecology and pollution but immorality and sin. 2 Peter 3:10–13 indicates that because of the world's pervasive evil, the Lord will one day destroy the universe and then create "new heavens and a new earth."

ADDITIONAL SCRIPTURES

- By faith we understand that the universe was created by the word of God, so that what is seen was not made out of things that are visible. (Hebrews 11:3 ESV)

- For in six days the LORD made the heavens and the earth, the sea, and all that is in them, but he rested on the seventh day. (Exodus 20:11 NIV)

- For thus says the LORD, who created the heavens (he is God!), who formed the earth and made it (he established it; he did not create it empty, he formed it to be inhabited!): "I am the LORD, and there is no other." (Isaiah 45:18 ESV)

WHAT OTHERS SAY

The soul's deepest thirst is for God Himself, who has made us so that we can never be satisfied without Him. *F. F. Bruce*

SO WHAT?

Revelation 4:11 states that God is worthy to receive honor because He has created everything. Let's consider how we can better offer our Creator the worship He deserves.

The World

IN TEN WORDS OR LESS
The world of unbelievers opposes God and needs His salvation.

DETAILS, PLEASE
In the Bible, "the world" sometimes refers to the material world, the earth (Acts 17:24). But the phrase is most frequently used to refer to the moral world of unbelievers living under Satan's deception, who oppose God and His people (1 John 5:19). This is the world that Jesus came to save. According to 1 John 2:15–17, believers are to avoid the world's unbelieving influence, which indicates a lack of love for the Father. John then described the world's preoccupation with evil desires of the old nature, covetousness and arrogance, ending by noting the world will eventually be destroyed while faithful believers will live forever.

ADDITIONAL SCRIPTURES
- For everyone born of God overcomes the world. This is the victory that has overcome the world, even our faith. (1 John 5:4 NIV)
- Pure religion and undefiled before God and the Father is this, To visit the fatherless and widows in their affliction, and to keep himself unspotted from the world. (James 1:27)
- For God so loved the world, that he gave his only begotten Son, that whosoever believeth in him should not perish, but have everlasting life. For God sent not his Son into the world to condemn the world; but that the world through him might be saved. (John 3:16–17)

WHAT OTHERS SAY
Christ's kingdom people are not to reflect the world, but they are to influence the world; they are to be in it but not of it. *John MacArthur*

SO WHAT?
Since Christ loved the world and came to save it through His sacrificial death, we must take His Gospel message to those who need it.

Light

IN TEN WORDS OR LESS
God is light and gives spiritual life, understanding, and truth.

DETAILS, PLEASE
In John 8:12 Jesus said, "I am the light of the world: he that followeth me shall not walk in darkness but shall have the light of life." Because of ancient prophecies such as those in Isaiah 9:2 and 42:6, the Jews longed for their Messiah to arrive on the scene, bringing illumination about truth, deliverance, and life. Jesus said that those following Him in obedient faith would no longer experience personal darkness—symbolic of ignorance, sin, and evil, which dominate an unregenerate life. They would enjoy the blessings of a new abundant life and understand God's truth.

ADDITIONAL SCRIPTURES
- For you were once darkness, but now you are light in the Lord. Live as children of light. (Ephesians 5:8 NIV)
- Ye should shew forth the praises of him who hath called you out of darkness into his marvellous light. (1 Peter 2:9)
- For God, who commanded the light to shine out of darkness, hath shined in our hearts, to give the light of the knowledge of the glory of God in the face of Jesus Christ. (2 Corinthians 4:6)
- Thy word is a lamp unto my feet, and a light unto my path. (Psalm 119:105)

WHAT OTHERS SAY
Consider the life you live—how do other people perceive your faith? While God doesn't expect you to live in perfection, He desires that you would do all you can to shine forth His light so others will see Him clearly. *Paul Chappell*

SO WHAT?
Jesus' disciples are the light of the world. We need to influence others by our good lives, words, and works—not drawing attention to ourselves but to the Father, so He may be glorified.

Miracles

Miracles are supernatural displays of God's power for His glory.

DETAILS, PLEASE

Biblical miracles occurred outside the normal boundaries of the laws of science.

Jesus' miracles resulted in verifiable physical healings of multitudes. Perhaps the greatest was Lazarus's resurrection, after he had been dead four days (John 11:38–44). In this story, Jesus let men assist Him by removing the stone from Lazarus's tomb's opening and removing his graveclothes. But only Jesus could raise the dead by saying, "Lazarus, come forth!"

In Acts 3–4 Jesus' apostles were involved in healing a paralyzed man, who stood for the first time, then walked, jumped, and praised God (3:7–9). This was front-page news, and in the following chapter, hostile, unbelieving religious leaders consulted together and agreed that they couldn't deny that a remarkable miracle had occurred (4:16).

Sometimes God's miraculous power also brought His righteous judgment against sin. This occurred in the days of Noah (Genesis 6–7) and during Israel's exodus from Egypt (Exodus 7–12). It is also anticipated for the end-times (Matthew 24:21; Revelation 6:15–17).

ADDITIONAL SCRIPTURES

- The signs of a true apostle were performed among you with utmost patience, with signs and wonders and mighty works. (2 Corinthians 12:12 ESV)
- Barnabas and Paul [declared] what miracles and wonders God had wrought among the Gentiles by them. (Acts 15:12)
- God also [testified] with them, both by signs and wonders, and by various miracles and by gifts of the Holy Spirit according to His own will. (Hebrews 2:4 NASB)
- "Fellow Israelites, listen to this: Jesus of Nazareth was a man accredited by God to you by miracles, wonders and signs, which God did among you through him, as you yourselves know." (Acts 2:22 NIV)

- You are the God who performs miracles; you display your power among the peoples. (Psalm 77:14 NIV)

WHAT OTHERS SAY

I never have any difficulty believing in miracles, since I experienced the miracle of a change in my own heart. *Augustine*

SO WHAT?

We should stand in awe of God, whose miracles bless His children and judge His enemies.

Scripture

IN TEN WORDS OR LESS

The Holy Scriptures are God's completed, written revelation for mankind.

DETAILS, PLEASE

In 2 Timothy 3 the apostle Paul exhorted Timothy to continue in the sacred writings that he had learned and trusted (verse 14). In these writings, he learned about salvation in Christ (verse 15).

In verses 16–17 Paul expressed the value, reliability, and authority of scripture by describing the method by which God gave His Word. He called it *inspiration*. The term means that God "breathed out" His Word. The point is that the scriptures find their ultimate source in divine rather than merely human origins. The Bible uses other titles to emphasize this truth: "the word *of God*" (1 Thessalonians 2:13, emphasis added) and "the oracles *of God*" (Romans 3:2, emphasis added).

It's critical to note that God's method of inspiring scripture was to select holy men who were directed by His Spirit to write down His words without error, but who also used their own individual vocabulary and writing style. The apostle Peter said that "holy men of God spake as they were moved by the Holy Ghost" (2 Peter 1:21).

Paul went on, in 2 Timothy 3:16, to indicate scripture's usefulness in four important areas. First, it's profitable in the area of *doctrine*. These are teachings that are right, our body of truths and doctrinal statements based in scripture.

Next, *reproof* refers to conviction from warnings in God's Word about things that are not right. The Bible's instructions help keep us off dangerous paths. Third, *correction* speaks of being restored, telling us how to get right with God through repentance, confession, and forsaking of sin. Finally, *instruction in righteousness* addresses the process of how we daily maintain Christian living and stay right with God.

Paul concluded by stating that these four areas are provided so "that the man of God may be perfect, thoroughly furnished unto all good works" (2 Timothy 3:17). Through God's Word, His servants are capable of doing all that God has called them to do.

ADDITIONAL SCRIPTURES

- Now the Berean Jews were of more noble character than those in Thessalonica, for they received the message with great eagerness and examined the Scriptures every day to see if what Paul said was true. (Acts 17:11 NIV)

- Above all, you must understand that no prophecy of Scripture came about by the prophet's own interpretation of things. For prophecy never had its origin in the human will, but prophets, though human, spoke from God as they were carried along by the Holy Spirit. (2 Peter 1:20–21 NIV)

- Then Philip opened his mouth, and began at the same scripture, and preached unto him Jesus. (Acts 8:35)

WHAT OTHERS SAY

The idea of *sola Scriptura* is that there is only one written source of divine revelation, which can never be placed on a parallel status with confessional statements, creeds, or the traditions of the church. Scripture alone has the authority to bind the conscience precisely because only scripture is the written revelation of almighty God. *R. C. Sproul*

SO WHAT?

Because God has been pleased to give us His completed Word, we should do our best to love it, learn it, and live it.

Revelation

IN TEN WORDS OR LESS
God reveals Himself to mankind that we might know Him.

DETAILS, PLEASE
If God did not reveal Himself, we would know nothing about Him. We would be left to our own imaginations, which leads to idolatrous ideas.

He reveals Himself through both "general revelation" and "special revelation." In general revelation, God's glory is seen in what He created. This is God's 24/7 global revelation, available to everyone in every language. As Psalm 19:1 says, "The heavens declare the glory of God."

In special revelation, God reveals Himself on the pages of scripture: "The law of the LORD is perfect, converting the soul: the testimony of the LORD is sure, making wise the simple (Psalm 19:7).

The very last book of the Bible is titled "the Revelation." It reveals truth about Jesus Christ's return to establish His eternal kingdom in a new heaven and new earth.

ADDITIONAL SCRIPTURES
- No man hath seen God at any time, the only begotten Son, which is in the bosom of the Father, he hath declared him. (John 1:18)
- For the wrath of God is revealed from heaven against all ungodliness and unrighteousness of men, who hold the truth in unrighteousness. Because that which may be known of God is manifest in them; for God hath shewed it unto them. (Romans 1:18–19)

WHAT OTHERS SAY
Bible reading enables us. . .to enjoy communion with God as He speaks to us from His Word, encouraging us, instructing us, and revealing Himself to us. *Jerry Bridges*

SO WHAT?
Jesus said that those who have truth revealed to them by the Father in heaven are especially blessed.

Truth

Truth is reality in light of God's nature and words.

DETAILS, PLEASE

The subject of truth must begin with God, who described Himself as "the LORD God, merciful and gracious, longsuffering, and abundant in goodness and truth" (Exodus 34:6). Through God's inspiration, Moses described Him as "a God of truth and without iniquity, just and right is he" (Deuteronomy 32:4). Jesus claimed, "I am the way, the truth, and the life: no man cometh unto the Father, but by me" (John 14:6), and He prayed for those who would follow Him, "that they might know thee the only true God, and Jesus Christ whom thou hast sent" (John 17:3).

Left to their own imagination, human beings turn away from truth into error. They arrive at evil conclusions that originate with the devil, the father of unbelievers who "was a murderer from the beginning, and abode not in the truth, because there is no truth in him" (John 8:44). Sinners who are converted are described as those who "turned to God from idols to serve the living and true God" (1 Thessalonians 1:9). Through the Holy Spirit's discernment, we can detect "the spirit of truth, and the spirit of error" (1 John 4:6).

God communicates His truth through His Son, Jesus Christ, and through the scriptures. Jesus said of John the Baptist that he "bare witness unto the truth" (John 5:33), directing people to Himself, the Lamb of God (John 1:29). Scripture emphasizes that truth is found in Jesus. In John 1 He is described as "the Word [who] was God. . .made flesh" (verses 1, 14). This Word "dwelt among us, (and we beheld his glory, the glory as of the only begotten of the Father,) full of grace and truth" (verse 14).

Jesus is also described by a contrast: "The law was given by Moses, but grace and truth came by Jesus Christ" (John 1:17). Comparatively speaking, the law of Moses is like reflected moonlight, but grace and truth, which came by Christ, shine like the brilliant sun. The New Testament ends with God's instructions to John: "Write: for these words are true" (Revelation 21:5).

ADDITIONAL SCRIPTURES

- And ye shall know the truth, and the truth shall make you free. (John 8:32)

- "But when he, the Spirit of truth, comes, he will guide you into all the truth. He will not speak on his own; he will speak only what he hears, and he will tell you what is yet to come." (John 16:13 NIV)

- Sanctify them through thy truth: thy word is truth. (John 17:17)

WHAT OTHERS SAY

Truth is what God thinks; it is what God does; it is what God is; it is what God has revealed of Himself in the Bible. Truth is found in its fullest form in God, for He is truth; He is the very source and origin of all truth. *Tim Challies*

SO WHAT?

Since God's truth is deposited in His written Word, we should spend our time and energy studying it.

Law

IN TEN WORDS OR LESS

"The law" encompasses all of God's rules for humanity.

DETAILS, PLEASE

Moses declared that no other nation had the advantage of such amazing laws as the ones that God provided to Israel (Deuteronomy 4:8). These laws expressed His will and were for the people's good (Deuteronomy 10:13). Their many laws were summarized into the Ten Commandments (Exodus 34:28) and condensed by Jesus into two great commandments about loving God and one's neighbor (Matthew 22:37–40). Since many misunderstood God's law, the apostle Paul clarified in Romans 3:20, "By the deeds of the law there shall no flesh be justified in his sight: for by the law is the knowledge of sin." Our attempts to obey the law do not save; they expose sin by showing how corrupt we are. Paul made it plain that only Jesus can save: "Knowing that a man is not justified by the works of the law, but by the faith of Jesus Christ, even we have believed in Jesus Christ" (Galatians 2:16).

ADDITIONAL SCRIPTURES

- The law is holy, and the commandment holy, and just, and good. (Romans 7:12)
- For whosoever shall keep the whole law, and yet offend in one point, he is guilty of all. (James 2:10)
- Christ is the end of the law for righteousness to every one that believeth. (Romans 10:4)

WHAT OTHERS SAY

In the maxims of the law, God is seen as the rewarder of perfect righteousness and the avenger of sin. But in Christ, His face shines out, full of grace and gentleness to poor, unworthy sinners. *John Calvin*

SO WHAT?

Believers realize that God's law is a thing of beauty, as the psalmist wrote: "O how love I thy law! it is my meditation all the day" (Psalm 119:97). But they really exult in the fact that Jesus fulfilled the law for them.

Covenants

IN TEN WORDS OR LESS

Covenants are God's promises that bring blessing to undeserving people.

DETAILS, PLEASE

God is the God of covenants in His relation to humanity. Covenants bind two parties together in an agreement involving promises and responsibilities. The first covenant in scripture, with Noah in Genesis 6:17–22, preserved humans and animals from the worldwide flood. In time another covenant, described in Genesis 12:1–3, was made with Abram. God promised to bless him, and in his seed the entire earth would be blessed. Centuries later God made a covenant with Moses and Israel that they would be God's "peculiar treasure. . .above all people" (Exodus 19:5). God then made a personal covenant with King David that he would have a descendant to rule forever; this would be fulfilled in Jesus (Luke 1:31–32). Finally, God spoke a new covenant, which brings full and free forgiveness to sinners through Christ (Jeremiah 31:31–33).

ADDITIONAL SCRIPTURES

- "This cup is the new covenant in my blood, which is poured out for you." (Luke 22:20 NIV)
- Now the God of peace, that brought again from the dead our Lord Jesus, that great shepherd of the sheep, through the blood of the everlasting covenant, make you perfect in every good work to do his will. (Hebrews 13:20–21)

WHAT OTHERS SAY

God is a covenant-making and covenant-keeping God. If you have never thought of Him in these terms, then you have not yet to think about Him in the way He wants you to. . . . In a sense the Bible is the book of His covenant. *Sinclair Ferguson*

SO WHAT?

The goal of God's covenants leads to the glorious future in Revelation 22 when people will live, serve, and reign with Him forever.

God's Will

IN TEN WORDS OR LESS

God's Will is what God wants people to know and do.

DETAILS, PLEASE

The subject of God's will falls into two major categories: the will of God that He has clearly revealed in scripture, which reveals His mind and heart, and God's will for individuals making personal life decisions. God has been clear about what has been called His moral will, revealed in scripture. Simply put, if we want to know God's will, we must learn God's Word, where His will is revealed. It's important to understand God's desire for sinners to know His great love for them. He said of himself that He "is longsuffering toward us, not willing that any should perish but that all should come to repentance" (2 Peter 3:9 NKJV).

Regarding doing God's will in Christian living, the apostle Paul encouraged believers to be thoughtful, saying, "Do not be foolish, but understand what the Lord's will is" (Ephesians 5:17 NIV). He continued instructing Christians to do "the will of God from the heart" (Ephesians 6:6) and to be concerned about being set apart (or sanctified) by developing a life of moral purity (1 Thessalonians 4:3). Christians are also instructed: "Rejoice evermore. Pray without ceasing. In every thing give thanks: for this is the will of God in Christ Jesus concerning you" (1 Thessalonians 5:16–18).

But how can we have a sense of God leading our personal lives into His plan and will for us? Counsel comes from the wise king Solomon: "Trust in the LORD with all thine heart; and lean not unto thine own understanding. In all thy ways acknowledge him, and he shall direct thy paths" (Proverbs 3:5–6).

Our personal trust in God's goodness and wisdom is vital to receive His leading. The temptation for many is trusting their own merely human thinking that disregards God's goodness and wisdom. The object of our pursuit should be counsel from God's Word: "Thy word is a lamp unto my feet, and a light unto my path" (Psalm 119:105). Everyone seeking God's will should learn this prayer: "Teach me to do your will, for you are my God! Let your good Spirit lead me on level ground!" (Psalm 143:10 ESV).

ADDITIONAL SCRIPTURES

- You need to persevere so that when you have done the will of God, you will receive what he has promised. (Hebrews 10:36 NIV)

- If any of you lacks wisdom, you should ask God, who gives generously to all without finding fault, and it will be given to you. (James 1:5 NIV)

- Thy kingdom come, thy will be done in earth, as it is in heaven. (Matthew 6:10)

- "O My Father, if it is possible, let this cup pass from Me; nevertheless, not as I will, but as You will." (Matthew 26:39 NKJV)

WHAT OTHERS SAY

Where love is the compelling power, there is no sense of strain or conflict or bondage in doing what is right: the man or woman who is compelled by Jesus' love and empowered by His Spirit does the will of God from the heart. *F. F. Bruce*

SO WHAT?

As our lives are quickly passing by, we should commit our remaining days to doing God's will.

Man

IN TEN WORDS OR LESS

God created mankind male and female, in His own image.

DETAILS, PLEASE

Mankind is the crown of God's creation since God made us super-naturally in His image and after His likeness (Genesis 1:26). We are the product of God's direct creation, possessing qualities that separate us from animals. We mirror God's image morally, spiritually, and intellectually through our intellect, emotion, and will. Jesus verified that God created man directly (Mark 10:6), as did the apostle Paul (Acts 17:26). Those first humans, Adam and Eve, fell into a state of sin and death, which was passed to all people (Romans 5:12). But God saves sinners and transforms believers, working through His Spirit and Word as "the new self. . .is being renewed in knowledge in the image of its Creator" (Colossians 3:10 NIV).

ADDITIONAL SCRIPTURES

- Then the LORD God formed a man from the dust of the ground and breathed into his nostrils the breath of life, and the man became a living being. (Genesis 2:7 NIV)

- Therefore we do not lose heart. Though outwardly we are wasting away, yet inwardly we are being renewed day by day. (2 Corinthians 4:16 NIV)

- O come, let us worship and bow down: let us kneel before the LORD our maker. (Psalm 95:6)

WHAT OTHERS SAY

I would rather be what God chose to make me than the most glorious creature that I could think of; for to have been thought about, born in God's thought, and then made by God, is the dearest, grandest, and most precious thing in all thinking. *George MacDonald*

SO WHAT?

When David compared the nighttime stars with man, he marveled at God's concern for us, asking "What is man. . .that you care for him?" (Psalm 8:4 ESV)

Marriage

IN TEN WORDS OR LESS

Marriage unites a man and woman to become one.

DETAILS, PLEASE

Marriage between a man and woman is a divinely ordained, life-long covenant of companionship based on mutual love for each other and the Lord. The apostle Paul revealed that marriage is a mysterious portrayal of the relationship between Christ and His church.

In Ephesians 5:22–33 Paul gave marital instructions to Christian families for the enjoyment of their union. Verses 22–24 instruct wives to help their husbands lead their families with loving support and cooperation. Verses 25–29 counsel husbands to develop sacrificial love similar to the love Jesus displayed at the cross when He gave Himself for His bride, the church. This should be a sanctifying love that seeks a wife's spiritual well-being (verse 26–27). Through loving relationships in marriages, husbands and wives can experience God's blessings "till death us do part."

ADDITIONAL SCRIPTURES

- Therefore a man shall leave his father and mother and be joined to his wife, and they shall become one flesh. (Genesis 2:24 NKJV)
- He who finds a wife finds what is good and receives favor from the Lord. (Proverbs 18:22 NIV)
- "So they are no longer two but one flesh. What therefore God has joined together, let not man separate." (Matthew 19:6 ESV)

WHAT OTHERS SAY

This institution points us to our hope of Christ returning to claim his bride, making marriage a living picture of the gospel of grace. *Christopher Ash*

SO WHAT?

When God unites two people in marriage, He also provides instructions in the "marriage manual" of His Word and His Spirit's power to produce joy in our homes.

Angels

IN TEN WORDS OR LESS

Angels are spiritual beings created to worship and serve God.

DETAILS, PLEASE

The study of angels is called angelology. Angels are mentioned in the Bible over 250 times. They are created beings called "spirits" (Hebrews 1:14) who are intelligent, powerful, and invisible. They were created simultaneously in a fixed innumerable figure described as "numbering myriads of myriads and thousands of thousands" (Revelation 5:11 ESV) that never increase (Matthew 22:30) or decrease (Luke 20:36). Their creation is not mentioned in Genesis 1, but Job 38:7 describes angels as "morning stars" and "sons of God" praising Him during the creation of the earth.

Not everyone believes that angels exist. During Jesus' ministry, the Sadducees denied the supernatural and rejected the existence of angels (Acts 23:8). Angels have the capability to temporarily appear in human form when it serves God's purposes so that some people, according to Hebrews 13:2, have even interacted with angels without realizing it! There is no biblical evidence for the belief that people become angels after they die.

Angels are divided into two fixed categories. The first category is the "holy angels" that are sinless and faithfully serve God (Mark 8:38). Two high-ranking angels are named in scripture: "Michael the archangel," who watches over Israel (Jude 9), and "Gabriel," a special angelic messenger who brought the birth announcement about Jesus (Luke 1:26). When Jesus was being arrested, He explained that twelve legions of combat-ready holy angels were prepared to come to His rescue if He requested their assistance (Matthew 26:53). Historians tell us that a Roman legion numbered six thousand soldiers, which means over seventy thousand powerful angels were available to aid Jesus if called.

The second category is called devil's angels (Matthew 25:41). In this group of evil angels many, who are also called "demons" (Matthew 12:28 NIV) and "unclean spirits" (Mark 5:13), actively oppose believers (Ephesians 6:12). A smaller group in this category is confined by God, awaiting future judgment (Jude 6).

Some people have been tempted with an unhealthy obsession about angels that has led to the idolatrous sin of worshipping angels (Colossians 2:18). Even the apostle John, who stood in the presence of a glorious angel, mistakenly offered him worship, only to be immediately corrected for this idolatry (Revelation 19:10).

A number of verses in Hebrews 1 describe angels. It's indicated that their primary function today as "ministering spirits" is providing aid to Christians (verse 14). We can thank God for the unseen help they provide!

ADDITIONAL SCRIPTURES

- Bless the Lord, ye his angels, that excel in strength, that do his commandments, hearkening unto the voice of his word. (Psalm 103:20)

- When the Son of man shall come in his glory, and all the holy angels with him, then shall he sit upon the throne of his glory. (Matthew 25:31)

- "There is joy before the angels of God over one sinner who repents." (Luke 15:10 esv)

WHAT OTHERS SAY

Few biblical topics have provoked more wild speculation. . .than the topic of angels. . . . It's important that we understand the biblical doctrine. . .correctly. . .when so much popular superstition surrounds and obscures the truth about these glorious creatures. *Phil Johnson*

SO WHAT?

Since angels can be our friends or foes, we should heed the warning of 1 John 4:1 (niv): "Do not believe every spirit, but test the spirits to see whether they are from God."

The Devil

IN TEN WORDS OR LESS

Satan is a powerful angelic enemy who seeks our destruction.

DETAILS, PLEASE

The devil's evil career began with his creation as a perfect angel. But his fall into evil is described in Ezekiel 28:12–17. He was involved in the fall of Adam and Eve, which brought ruin and death to mankind (Genesis 3). He now bears names that reveal his evil character: "the devil," meaning "slanderer" (Matthew 4:1); "the tempter" (Matthew 4:3); "Satan," meaning "adversary" (Matthew 4:10); "evil one" (Matthew 13:19 ESV); "father of [lies]" and "murderer" (John 8:44). In Revelation 12:9 he's "that old serpent" who deceives the whole world. Satan does all he can to keep people lost and in darkness (Matthew 13:38–39; 2 Corinthians 4:3–4). Christians can only overcome this enemy with God's help (Ephesians 6:10–18; James 4:7; 1 John 2:13).

Happily, there is good news. Jesus' ultimate defeat and removal of Satan is recorded in Revelation 20:10.

ADDITIONAL SCRIPTURES

- The God of peace will soon crush Satan under your feet. The grace of our Lord Jesus be with you. (Romans 16:20 NIV)

- Submit yourselves therefore to God. Resist the devil, and he will flee from you. (James 4:7)

- Whoever makes a practice of sinning is of the devil, for the devil has been sinning from the beginning. The reason the Son of God appeared was to destroy the works of the devil. (1 John 3:8 ESV)

WHAT OTHERS SAY

Satan's greatest success is in making people think they have plenty of time before they die to consider their eternal welfare. *John Owen*

SO WHAT?

Though Satan has power in this earth, it is not unlimited. God is stronger than he and will help us overcome his influence on our lives.

Sin

IN TEN WORDS OR LESS

Sin is every human nonconformance to God's holy standard.

DETAILS, PLEASE

In three psalms, David spoke of experiencing sin's disastrous effects—but also of discovering God's gracious forgiveness.

Psalm 51 is David's confession of sin. The inscription names key people involved in an incident of deceit, adultery, and murder. David's confession was months after his sin had been exposed. He began by appealing to God's love and mercy as the basis for forgiveness (verse 1). He then asked that his sin be removed, describing it as "transgressions" (emphasizing intentional rebellion), "iniquity" (referring to the perversion of twisting truth), and "sin" (meaning to fall short of a target). He admitted that he was haunted by sin's presence and recognized that his sin was ultimately against God. David even acknowledged his condition as a sinner since birth (verse 5) and knew that animal sacrifices offered to God on altars must be accompanied by his own humble sacrifice of a "broken spirit. . .and a contrite heart" (verse 17).

Psalm 32 is about David's joy and blessedness of being forgiven by God. He began in verses 1 and 2 (NKJV) by saying that his "transgression is forgiven" and his "sin is covered." Happily, "the LORD does not impute iniquity" [assign blame] to this blessed man. In verses 3 and 4, David described the unpleasant physical and mental effects of hiding his sin, but through honest and thorough confession, he received forgiveness (verse 5). His story can help us to deal with personal sins (verses 6–10).

Finally, in Psalm 19:12–14 are David's prayer requests about overcoming remaining sin in his life. In verse 12 he prayed for pardon for his blind spots that kept him from recognizing certain sins, and in verse 13 he asked that his known sins would not dominate him. His final request, in verse 14, was for purity in his thoughts and words. David called the Lord his "Rock," who provides strength against sin, and his "Redeemer," who sets people free from their sin.

ADDITIONAL SCRIPTURES

- "The Lord knows those who are His," and, "Let everyone who names the name of Christ depart from iniquity." (2 Timothy 2:19 NKJV)

- If we walk in the light, as he is in the light, we have fellowship with one another, and the blood of Jesus Christ his Son cleanseth us from all sin. (1 John 1:7)

WHAT OTHERS SAY

Sin is anything that violates the moral law of the universe. Anytime we do what God tells us not to do or fail to do what God commands us to do, we commit a sin. And every time we sin, we are found guilty in the sight of God and deserve divine judgment. *Philip Graham Ryken*

SO WHAT?

Like other believers who have run life's race victoriously, Christians today should be cautious about being entangled by sin and look to Jesus, their ultimate example.

Idolatry

IN TEN WORDS OR LESS
Idolatry sinfully places other things where only God should be.

DETAILS, PLEASE
The Ten Commandments, which reveal God's holy character, begin with prohibitions against the sin of idolatry, which is worshipping false gods instead of the one true God. He said, "You shall have no other gods before me. You shall not make for yourself an image in the form of anything in heaven above or on the earth beneath or in the waters below. You shall not bow down to them or worship them; for I, the LORD your God, am a jealous God" (Exodus 20:3–6 NIV).

The living God who revealed Himself to Moses requires first place in our lives. All rival false gods should be rejected, and all efforts to depict an image of our true God should be abandoned, since it is impossible to accurately characterize Him. God protects our relationship with Him by His holy jealousy—His zealous devotion to His people (Exodus 34:14).

ADDITIONAL SCRIPTURES
- Little children, keep yourselves from idols. (1 John 5:21)
- Ye turned to God from idols to serve the living and true God. (1 Thessalonians 1:9)
- If you ever forget the LORD your God and follow other gods and worship and bow down to them, I testify against you today that you will surely be destroyed. (Deuteronomy 8:19 NIV)

WHAT OTHERS SAY
You don't have to go to heathen lands today to find false gods. America is full of them. Whatever you love more than God is your idol. *D. L. Moody*

SO WHAT?
Tearing down idols in our lives involves honestly identifying and rejecting what has replaced the one true God's first place in our hearts. Christ alone must then be exalted as our first love.

Temptation

IN TEN WORDS OR LESS

Temptation is enticement to evil, from our hearts and Satan.

DETAILS, PLEASE

James 1 examines difficulties in the Christian life by considering trials designed by God for our good (verses 2–12), then ruinous temptations to evil (verses 13–15). While it is true that Satan, called "the tempter," will try to entice us to do wrong (he tried to trip up Jesus Himself in Matthew 4:1–11), James indicated that some of our temptations will come from deep inside ourselves: "Every man is tempted, when he is drawn away of his own lust, and enticed" (James 1:14). For encouragement in fighting temptation, we should anticipate God's future reward of a "crown of life" (verse 12). Until that day, we should never blame our temptations on God (verse 13). He gives only good and perfect gifts (verse 17).

ADDITIONAL SCRIPTURES

- For we have not an high priest which cannot be touched with the feeling of our infirmities; but was in all points tempted like as we are, yet without sin. (Hebrews 4:15)
- No temptation has overtaken you that is not common to man. God is faithful, and he will not let you be tempted beyond your ability, but with the temptation he will also provide the way of escape, that you may be able to endure it. (1 Corinthians 10:13 ESV)

WHAT OTHERS SAY

To be tempted is in itself no sin. It is the yielding to the temptation, and giving it a place in our hearts, which we must fear. *J. C. Ryle*

SO WHAT?

Jesus felt the full force of temptation yet remained sinless. During our temptations, we can run to Him for help.

Death

IN TEN WORDS OR LESS

Death is a penalty we earned with our sin.

DETAILS, PLEASE

God warned Adam about sin's death penalty (Genesis 2:17). Adam and Eve died spiritually the day they sinned and physically years later (Genesis 5:5). They had been created from the earth's ground, to which they would return (Genesis 3:19; Ecclesiastes 12:7). This death curse passed to everyone born after them (Romans 5:12). As Romans 6:23 says, "The wages of sin is death," and these wages are paid to everyone. Current global statistics state that 120 people die every minute.

Scripture describes three types of death.

1. Physical death: a separation of the soul from the body. James 2:26 explains that "the body without the spirit is dead." In death the soul leaves the body and the dead are called "the departed"; Genesis 35:18 (ESV) describes Rachel's death by saying "her soul was departing (for she was dying)."

2. Spiritual death: a separation of the soul from the life of God. This person is alive physically but dead spiritually, "being alienated from the life of God" (Ephesians 4:18) and "dead in trespasses and sins" (Ephesians 2:1). Because all are sinners (Romans 3:23), everyone is born spiritually dead.

3. Eternal death: a separation of guilty sinners from God in hell. It's called "the second death" in Revelation 2:11 (see also Revelation 20:12–15); the physical and spiritual death described above, when considered together, are the *first* death. Eternal death is a conscious consignment of unbelievers, called "the wicked" in scripture, to hell. Many oppose this divine judgment, suggesting that it is contrary to God's loving nature, but since this is the consequence of sin against the infinitely holy God, this punishment matches the crime (Romans 2:5).

God gives believers encouragement when facing death. Fear can be removed because of the Good Shepherd's promised presence (Psalm 23:4) and replaced with hope (Proverbs 14:32) and comfort (1 Thessalonians 4:13–18). Paradise is promised on the day of one's death (Luke 23:43). The victory of resurrection life is guaranteed: "There shall be no more death, nor sorrow, nor crying. There shall be no more pain (Revelation 21:4 NKJV), rather, incorruption and immortality (1 Corinthians 15:53). Until then we can pray, "Teach us to number our days, that we may apply our hearts unto wisdom" (Psalm 90:12).

ADDITIONAL SCRIPTURES

- "Blessed are the dead who die in the Lord from now on."
- "Yes" says the Spirit, "they will rest from their labor, for their deeds will follow them." (Revelation 14:13 NIV)
- For me to live is Christ, and to die is gain. (Philippians 1:21)
- Precious in the sight of the LORD is the death of his saints. (Psalm 116:15)

WHAT OTHERS SAY

Let us consider this settled, that no one has made progress in the school of Christ who does not joyfully await the day of death and final resurrection. *John Calvin*

SO WHAT?

The prospect of dying troubles some, but believers are hard-pressed between the good of remaining alive to serve Christ and departing to be with Christ, which is far better (Philippians 1:23).

Life

IN TEN WORDS OR LESS

God offers the gift of eternal life through Jesus Christ.

DETAILS, PLEASE

In the Bible, life (Greek: *zōē*) can refer to several things: (1) physical life received at conception (Psalm 51:5; 139:13–16); (2) spiritual life received through the new birth (being "born again"), resulting in "eternal life" as a present possession (John 3:15–16; 1 John 5:11–12); and (3) believers receiving future physical resurrection life after death (John 11:25). Jesus described spiritual life as an abundant experience filled with God's blessings (John 10:10). The apostle Paul explained the new birth as "the washing of regeneration" in Titus 3:5, not received because of our works but by God's mercy. And Jesus said, "I am the way, the truth, and the life. No one comes the Father except through Me" (John 14:6 NKJV). He gives this life to anyone who will humbly receive it (John 10:27–28).

ADDITIONAL SCRIPTURES

- He that heareth my word, and believeth on him that sent me, hath everlasting life, and shall not come into condemnation; but is passed from death unto life. (John 5:24)
- For the wages of sin is death; but the gift of God is eternal life through Jesus Christ our Lord. (Romans 6:23)

WHAT OTHERS SAY

Eternal life refers not only to eternal quantity but divine quality of life. It means literally "life of the age to come" and refers therefore to resurrection and heavenly existence in perfect glory and holiness. *John MacArthur*

SO WHAT?

Believers can enjoy abundant life now as they await, with sure hope, the forever life with Christ in glory.

Heaven

IN TEN WORDS OR LESS

Heaven is where God lives with the redeemed and angels.

DETAILS, PLEASE

The apostle Paul was a good person to talk about heaven, since he had the privilege of visiting before living there! He spoke about this in 2 Corinthians 12, explaining that he had been "caught up to the third heaven" (verse 2). It is best to understand the first heaven as the sky that's filled with clouds and birds (Genesis 1:8; 8:2), and the second heaven as outer space, filled with stars, planets, and galaxies (Genesis 15:5; Psalm 8:3–4). The third heaven is God's sanctuary (Psalm 123:1) that Jesus called "my Father's house" (John 14:2). There are "many dwelling places" (NASB) there. These heavenly dwellings will be personal, plentiful, permanent, and pleasing.

ADDITIONAL SCRIPTURES

- "However, do not rejoice that spirits submit to you, but rejoice that your names are written in heaven." (Luke 10:20 NIV)
- "You alone are the LORD; You have made heaven, the heaven of heavens, with all their host, the earth and everything on it, the seas and all that is in them, and You preserve them all. The host of heaven worships You." (Nehemiah 9:6 NKJV)

WHAT OTHERS SAY

I know that Christ is all in all; and that it is the presence of God that makes heaven to be heaven. But yet it much sweetens the thoughts of that place to me that there are there such a multitude of my most dear and precious friends in Christ. *Richard Baxter*

SO WHAT?

Christians should have great expectation because their "citizenship is in heaven" (Philippians 3:20 NIV). Our names are "written in heaven" (Hebrews 12:23), and we have an inheritance "reserved in heaven" for us (1 Peter 1:4)!

Hell

IN TEN WORDS OR LESS

Hell is where the holy God administers righteous judgment.

DETAILS, PLEASE

In Matthew 25:32 (NIV) Jesus described a future scene of God judging "all nations. . .gathered before Him." Contrary to many people's wishes, no one "will escape the judgment of God" (Romans 2:3 NKJV). His final verdicts are summarized in Matthew 25:46 (NKJV): some "will go away into everlasting punishment, but the righteous into eternal life." Both destinies are described as never ending. In verse 30 Jesus ended a parable describing hell as a place of regret, sorrow, and painful agony where some are cast "into outer darkness" to hear "weeping and gnashing of teeth."

The judged are banished forever from all of God's good blessings. Jesus will give this tragic command: "Depart from me, ye cursed" (Matthew 25:41). Sadly, because they reject Jesus in this life, they will be consigned to a place that was "prepared for the devil and his angels."

ADDITIONAL SCRIPTURES

- "Do not be afraid of those who kill the body but cannot kill the soul. Rather, be afraid of the One who can destroy both soul and body in hell." (Matthew 10:28 NIV)
- Thou art Peter, and upon this rock I will build my church; and the gates of hell shall not prevail against it. (Matthew 16:18)

WHAT OTHERS SAY

Significantly, of the twelve times the word *gehenna* [hell] is used in the New Testament, eleven times it came from the mouth of our Lord. Indeed, He spoke more about hell than heaven. *Erwin Lutzer*

SO WHAT?

God wants us to experience His salvation through Christ rather than His justice and wrath. We should heed the warning to "flee from the wrath to come" (Luke 3:7).

Israel

God's chosen people is the source of salvation for all.

DETAILS, PLEASE

Israel's name is found in the Bible over two thousand times. Their story began with God choosing Abraham, through whom He would bless the world through Christ (Galatians 3:6–9, 16). The Lord chose Abraham and his offspring "to be a people for Himself, a special treasure above all the peoples on the face of the earth. The LORD did not set His love on you nor choose you because you were more in number than any other people, for you were the least of all peoples; but because the LORD loves you, and because He would keep the oath which He swore to your fathers" (Deuteronomy 7:6–8 NKJV).

God provided a name change to Abraham's son, from *Jacob* (meaning "a deceiver") to *Israel*—"a prince with God" (Genesis 32:28; 35:9–10). Israel had twelve sons whose descendants became the twelve tribes of Israel, which were distinct from all other nations. In addition to this ethnic distinction was a spiritual one. As the apostle Paul said, "They are not all Israel who are of Israel" (Romans 9:6–7 NKJV). Abraham's true heirs, the recipients of God's promises, are those who experience God's saving work in their hearts by trusting Jesus Christ (Romans 2:28–29; 3:21–22).

ADDITIONAL SCRIPTURES

- Surely God is good to Israel, to those who are pure in heart. (Psalm 73:1 NIV)
- Therefore let all the house of Israel know assuredly, that God hath made the same Jesus, whom ye have crucified, both Lord and Christ. (Acts 2:36)

WHAT OTHERS SAY

The Pentateuch revealed that God chose Abraham, Isaac, and Jacob, and promised to bring the Messiah and Savior through their descendants. God promised to bless all nations through the seed of Abraham, which is Christ. *Steven Cole*

SO WHAT?

Israel pictures God's people who trust in Him.

Gospel

IN TEN WORDS OR LESS

Gospel is the good news of Jesus Christ bringing salvation.

DETAILS, PLEASE

The apostle Paul began 1 Corinthians 15, his "resurrection chapter," by discussing important details about the Gospel message. He said in verses 1–2 that he *preached* it, and that the Corinthian believers personally *received* it, *stood* in it, and were *saved* from their sins by it. By mentioning their salvation, he assured them that he accepted them as fellow Christians who had true saving faith, calling them "brethren." But he also warned about a possible problem in some who only displayed "vain" (superficial and worthless) faith. The Weymouth New Testament translates this "unless. . .your faith has been unreal from the very first." The author of Hebrews raised this serious concern, indicating that some people hear the Gospel but don't benefit from it because they lack true saving faith (Hebrews 4:2). Jesus and the apostles also expressed this concern in their teaching (Matthew 7:22–23; John 2:23–24; James 2:26).

First Corinthians 15:3–4 defines essential features of the Gospel. First, that "Christ died for our sins according to the scriptures." The Old Testament foretold Jesus' sacrificial death in Isaiah 53:4–6. Jesus' contemporary Mark confirmed the historical fact of His death, saying that He "breathed his last" on the cross (Mark 15:37 NIV). Roman soldiers who executed Jesus verified His death by piercing His side (John 19:34). His body then went through the customary Jewish burial process. As a final proof that Jesus really was dead, "he was buried" (1 Corinthians 15:4) by friends. Ultimately, His tomb was sealed with a large stone (John 19:38–42; Matthew 27:60).

The next Gospel feature, in 1 Corinthians 15:4, was that Jesus "rose again the third day according to the scriptures." This revealed His power over death and the fact that God had accepted His sacrificial death. His resurrection was predicted in Isaiah 53:10–12 and prefigured in the experience of the prophet Jonah (Matthew 12:38–41; Jonah 1:17). Eyewitness verification supported the fact that Jesus had risen, for He was seen by His twelve disciples, by five hundred brethren at once, and finally by all the apostles, including Paul (1 Corinthians 15:5–8).

Whoever brings these "good tidings of great joy. . .to all people" (Luke 2:10)—this Gospel of God's grace (Acts 20:24), the gospel of peace (Ephesians 6:15), and gospel of hope (Colossians 1:23)—are viewed as messengers with "beautiful feet" because of their beautiful message (Romans 10:15).

ADDITIONAL SCRIPTURES

- For I am not ashamed of the gospel of Christ, for it is the power of God to salvation for everyone who believes: for the Jew first and also for the Greek. (Romans 1:16 NKJV)
- Only let your manner of life be worthy of the gospel of Christ, so that whether I come and see you or am absent, I may hear of you that you are standing firm in one spirit, with one mind striving side by side for the faith of the gospel. (Philippians 1:27 ESV)

WHAT OTHERS SAY

The gospel is so simple that small children can understand it, and it is so profound that studies by the wisest theologians will never exhaust its riches. *Charles Hodge*

SO WHAT?

Having heard the Gospel, accept it. Having accepted it, share it! Be like the apostle Paul, who said, "Woe is me if I do not preach the gospel!" (1 Corinthians 9:16 NKJV).

Salvation

IN TEN WORDS OR LESS

Jesus Christ graciously rescues sinners through His death and resurrection.

DETAILS, PLEASE

People must realize that they are sinners needing God's salvation. Jesus explained the purpose of His incarnation as a great rescue mission: "I came not to call the righteous, but sinners to repentance" (Luke 5:32). He challenged those who didn't view themselves as sinners, describing a tax collector who humbly prayed with faith, "God be merciful to me a sinner," who was saved (Luke 18:13–14). Jesus explained to Zacchaeus that He had come "to seek and to save that which was lost" (Luke 19:10). To prove mankind's universal guilt, the apostle Paul quoted Psalm 14 as an Old Testament proof text that "there is none that doeth good, no, not one" (Romans 3:12).

Salvation has both positive and negative aspects. In John 3, where Jesus explained salvation to Nicodemus, we see that believers who trust in Christ's sacrificial death receive "eternal life" and are "saved" (verses 15, 17). But those who reject Jesus "perish," are condemned, and experience "the wrath of God" (verses 15, 18, 36). Paul further explained salvation in Romans 10, saying that it is available to everyone: "For whosoever shall call upon the name of the Lord shall be saved" (verse 13).

Because most things in life are gained through human achievement, many mistakenly think this is also true of salvation. Paul repeatedly corrected this idea, explaining that salvation is received by faith alone, through God's mercy and free grace. In Romans 4:1–8 he cited the examples of Abraham and David, who were not justified by works that created a debt owed to them as a reward; they only believed and were counted as righteous. Paul said similar things in Ephesians 2:8–9 and Titus 3:4–7.

For any believers struggling with doubts about their salvation, the apostle John said they could enjoy assurance by trusting God's promises (1 John 5:12). He also gave a series of tests revealing evidence of God's saving work in a person's life: the moral test of obedience (1 John 2:3–5), the social test of brotherly love (3:10–14), and the doctrinal test about Christ (4:15; 5:1). John concluded by saying, "These things have I written unto you that believe...that *ye may know* that ye have eternal life" (5:13, emphasis added).

ADDITIONAL SCRIPTURES

- There is no God else beside me; a just God and a Saviour; there is none beside me. Look unto me, and be ye saved, all the ends of the earth: for I am God, and there is none else. (Isaiah 45:21–22)

- Here is a trustworthy saying that deserves full acceptance: Christ Jesus came into the world to save sinners—of whom I am the worst. (1 Timothy 1:15 NIV)

- Let all those that seek thee rejoice and be glad in thee: let such as love thy salvation say continually, The LORD be magnified. (Psalm 40:16)

WHAT OTHERS SAY

As a result of grace, we have been saved from sin's penalty. One day we will be saved from sin's presence. In the meantime, we are being saved from sin's power. *Alistair Begg*

SO WHAT?

Since God doesn't want anyone to perish (2 Peter 3:9), all believers should be laborers together with God to win the lost.

Crucifixion

IN TEN WORDS OR LESS

On the cross, Jesus paid the price for our sins.

DETAILS, PLEASE

During New Testament times, crucifixion was the Roman Empire's method of public execution. Jesus' crucifixion is portrayed in all four Gospels.

Jesus had tried to prepare His disciples for the terrible sufferings He would face on the cross (Matthew 16:21). In spite of the shocking injustice of the Roman court system, driven by mob pressure (John 19:4–16), Jesus gave reassurance that His death was voluntary (John 10:17–18) and substitutionary (Mark 10:45). He gave Himself in our place so we could be freed from sin.

Jesus was crucified between two criminals with differing opinions about Him. One man sought only release from his execution, while the other sought the salvation of his soul. Jesus promised him, "Today you will be with me in paradise" (Luke 23:43 NIV).

The Lord's death is remembered today in the Communion ritual described in 1 Corinthians 11:23–26. Jesus said, "Do this in remembrance of me" (verse 24 NIV).

ADDITIONAL SCRIPTURES

- But we preach Christ crucified, unto the Jews a stumbling block, and unto the Greeks foolishness. (1 Corinthians 1:23)
- I am crucified with Christ: nevertheless I live; yet not I, but Christ liveth in me: and the life which I now live in the flesh I live by the faith of the Son of God, who loved me, and gave himself for me. (Galatians 2:20)

WHAT OTHERS SAY

Until you see the cross as that which is done by you, you will never appreciate that it is done for you. *John Stott*

SO WHAT?

Jesus, our sinless substitute, bore our sins in His body so we could die to sin and live righteously for Him who has healed us (1 Peter 2:24).

Sacrifice

IN TEN WORDS OR LESS
Sacrifices are acts of worship or service offered to God.

DETAILS, PLEASE
Animal sacrifice began early in human history (see Genesis 4:3–4). Israel's original Passover observance involved the death of acceptable animals whose blood was applied to the doorposts of homes for protection from judgment (Exodus 12:13–14). The sacrifices on Israel's national Day of Atonement, Yom Kippur, were for all the nation's sins (Leviticus 16:1–34). Animal sacrifices could not remove sins but provided a temporary covering, as well as the shadow of complete forgiveness anticipating Jesus, the Lamb of God, who takes away sin. His death brought an end to animal sacrifices (Hebrews 10:1–4; 11–14, 19–22).

Christians today are considered priests offering God "spiritual sacrifices, acceptable to God by Jesus Christ" (1 Peter 2:5). This includes serving God as a "living sacrifice," doing His will (Romans 12:1), offering Him our finances to support missions (Philippians 4:17–18), and offering Him our praise, thanksgiving, and good works. We're told that "with such sacrifices God is well pleased" (Hebrews 13:16).

ADDITIONAL SCRIPTURES
- For even Christ our passover is sacrificed for us. (1 Corinthians 5:7)
- "Does the LORD delight in burnt offerings and sacrifices as much as in obeying the LORD? To obey is better than sacrifice, and to heed is better than the fat of rams." (1 Samuel 15:22 NIV)

WHAT OTHERS SAY
If Jesus Christ be God and died for me, then no sacrifice can be too great for me to make for Him. *C. T. Studd*

SO WHAT?
God prefers our obedience to our confessions. He said, "To do righteousness and justice is desired by the LORD more than sacrifice" (Proverbs 21:3 NASB).

Atonement

IN TEN WORDS OR LESS

Atonement describes God removing man's guilt through blood sacrifice.

DETAILS, PLEASE

The term *atonement* appears repeatedly in the Old Testament, indicating man's need for reconciliation with God through sacrifice. The necessity of blood sacrifice providing substitutionary atonement for sinners is explained in Leviticus 17:11: "For the life of the flesh is in the blood: and I have given it to you upon the altar to make an atonement for your souls." Since animal sacrifices were insufficient to permanently remove sin, they required repeating (Hebrews 10:11).

The King James Version New Testament only uses the word *atonement* once, in Romans 5:11. But in New Testament theology, atonement has been expanded to express the total significance of Christ's death with biblical words like *reconciliation, redemption, justification,* and *propitiation*: "Behold the Lamb of God, which *taketh away* the sin of the world" (John 1:29, emphasis added).

ADDITIONAL SCRIPTURES

God presented Christ as a sacrifice of atonement, through the shedding of his blood—to be received by faith. He did this to demonstrate his righteousness, because in his forbearance he had left the sins committed beforehand unpunished. (Romans 3:25 NIV)

He did not enter by means of the blood of goats and calves; but he entered by the Most Holy Place once for all by his own blood, thus obtaining eternal redemption. (Hebrews 9:12 NIV)

WHAT OTHERS SAY

In the Gospel there is declared. . .unto sinners an *absolute free pardon* of all their sins, without any satisfaction or compensation made. . .by themselves—namely, on the account of the atonement made for them by Jesus Christ. *John Owen*

SO WHAT?

The solemn Christian ceremony of Communion remembers the sacrifice Jesus made for His people. It must always be done in a respectful manner.

Reconciliation

IN TEN WORDS OR LESS

Friendship with God is offered through Christ's death.

DETAILS, PLEASE

In 2 Corinthians 5:17–21 the apostle Paul discusses *reconciliation*, meaning "to change" or "exchange." This text describes God's saving work of changing people's hostilities toward Him so they can become united to Him as those made new in Christ (verse 17). God first reconciles people to Himself (verses 18–19), not holding them accountable for their sins—He is "not imputing their trespasses unto them." *Impute* is a banking term meaning "to put on one's account." The punishment for sin has been paid in full, removed from the sinner's account and applied to Christ in the great exchange (verse 21). Once reconciled, Christ's former enemies become His "ambassadors" (verse 20)—official diplomats acting with "the ministry of reconciliation" (verse 18) and speaking on His behalf with "the word of reconciliation" (verse 19). Christians are supposed to reach others with the message "Be ye reconciled to God" (verse 20). This message is one of great urgency. As Paul wrote in the next chapter, "Now is the day of salvation" (6:2)!

ADDITIONAL SCRIPTURES

- For if, when we were enemies, we were reconciled to God by the death of his Son, much more, being reconciled, we shall be saved by his life. (Romans 5:10)

- For He Himself is our peace, who has made both one, and has broken down the middle wall of separation. (Ephesians 2:14 NKJV)

WHAT OTHERS SAY

There can be no peace between you and Christ while there is peace between you and sin. *Charles. H. Spurgeon*

SO WHAT?

Since God through the Gospel has removed the former hostility between us and Him, we should remove hostilities between ourselves and others so people can find their way to Him.

Redemption

IN TEN WORDS OR LESS

Redemption means rescuing from captivity by paying a price.

DETAILS, PLEASE

Redemption is an ancient theme describing rescue from dire circumstances by a capable redeemer. Two Old Testament stories illustrate the meaning. The first is Israel's national liberation from Egyptian slavery by the Lord their Redeemer (Exodus 6:6–8). Then the book of Ruth addresses personal redemption under Mosaic laws by a kinsman-redeemer, a family champion appointed to rescue family members in need, as defined in Leviticus 25:25–27. The widow Ruth struggled under life's hardships until she placed herself in a humbling position that let her willing relative, Boaz, know how desperately she needed him to become her kinsman-redeemer (Ruth 3:9–11).

In the New Testament, the apostle Peter uses redemption language to describe sinners, once enslaved to sin but now set free by Jesus Christ, who willingly paid the ransom for them by His sacrificial death. They now belong to Him (1 Peter 1:15–21).

1 Peter 1:18–19 presents a contrast, revealing the infinite price paid for our redemption. "Silver and gold" had no place in this transaction. The required ransom price was "the precious blood of Christ, a lamb without blemish or defect" (NIV). Jesus said that He came "to give His life a ransom for many" (Mark 10:45). The apostle Paul added that this redemption was "according to the riches of [God's] grace" (Ephesians 1:7).

Peter again, in 1 Peter 1:20–21, describes Christ's redeeming work as being planned by God before creation and appearing in history "*for you*" (emphasis added). God's actions become very personal. Christ's death, resurrection, and ascension to glory are so that our "faith and hope might be in God."

Isaiah prophesied about the world's future recognition of God our Redeemer: "All flesh shall know that I the Lord am thy Saviour and thy Redeemer, the mighty One of Jacob" (Isaiah 49:26). The suffering Job acknowledged God's redemption by saying, "I know that my Redeemer lives, and He shall stand at last on the earth; and after my skin is destroyed, this I know, that in my flesh I shall see God" (Job 19:25–26 NKJV).

ADDITIONAL SCRIPTURES

- [Jesus Christ] gave himself for us to redeem us from all wickedness and purify for himself a people that are his very own, eager to do what is good. (Titus 2:14 NIV)

- But God will redeem my soul from the power of the grave: for he shall receive me. Selah. (Psalm 49:15)

- For ye are bought with a price: therefore glorify God in your body, and in your spirit, which are God's. (1 Corinthians 6:20)

WHAT OTHERS SAY

Great was the work of creation, but greater was the work of redemption. It cost more to redeem us than to make us. In the one there was but the speaking of the Word; in the other there was the shedding of blood. The creation was but the work of God's fingers (Psalm 8:3). Redemption is the work of His arm (Luke 1:51). *Thomas Watson*

SO WHAT?

As we recognize that we belong to God, who willingly purchased us at an infinite price, we should sing to our Redeemer with joyful praise (Psalm 71:23).

Justification

IN TEN WORDS OR LESS

Justification means God declares the guilty righteous through Christ.

DETAILS, PLEASE

In Romans 3:9–20, the apostle Paul discusses mankind's need for justification. He begins by establishing humanity's guilt with a devastating indictment (verses 10–11), announcing a final verdict in verse 19: "All the world [is] guilty before God." He then corrects peoples' most common misconception about their own good works, saying, "by the deeds of the law no flesh will be justified in [God's] sight, for by the law is the knowledge of sin" (verse 20 NKJV). The law doesn't function like a ladder for us to work our way to God—it is more like a mirror, revealing our sin and need.

The solution to this problem is found in Romans 3:21–31. Believing sinners are "justified freely by His grace through the redemption that is in Christ Jesus" (verse 24 NKJV). The "law of faith" (3:27) eliminates people's bragging about their own efforts to earn salvation (see Romans 4:1–2). We now boast in Jesus' work on the cross (Galatians 6:14–15).

ADDITIONAL SCRIPTURES

- "I tell you that this man, rather than the other, went home justified before God. For all those who exalt themselves will be humbled, and those who humble themselves will be exalted." (Luke 18:14 NIV)

- Now it is evident that no one is justified before God by the law, for "The righteous shall live by faith." (Galatians 3:11 ESV)

WHAT OTHERS SAY

A not guilty is entered into the court of God when this blood is pleaded, and a not guilty inscribed upon the roll of conscience when this blood is sprinkled. *Stephen Charnock*

SO WHAT?

By being justified by faith in Christ, believers possess peace with God. This is the greatest peace available to man.

Imputation

Imputation gives credit or assigns blame to someone else.

DETAILS, PLEASE

This banking term means "to put to one's account," like money deposited. The concept is illustrated by Israel's high priests, who laid hands on the head of sacrificial animals, symbolically transferring (imputing) man's sins to the creatures (Leviticus 16:21–22). God imputed (credited) righteousness to Abraham (Romans 4:1–4) and to David (verses 5–8) by faith alone, apart from works.

The apostle Paul spoke of three major imputations—first, Adam's sin passed to all his descendants (Romans 5:12–14) whose "righteousnesses are as filthy rags" (Isaiah 64:6). Second, believers' sin is charged to Christ as their sin bearer. And third, Christ's righteousness is credited to believers for a new standing before God (2 Corinthians 5:21). They can testify, "My soul shall be joyful in my God; for He has clothed me with the garments of salvation, He has covered me with the robe of righteousness" (Isaiah 61:10 NKJV).

ADDITIONAL SCRIPTURES

- Blessed is the man to whom the LORD does not impute iniquity, and in whose spirit there is no deceit. (Psalm 32:2 NKJV)
- If he has wronged you at all, or owes you anything, charge that to my account. (Philemon 18 ESV)

WHAT OTHERS SAY

For myself, 2 Corinthians 5:21 is enough, affirming the glorious exchange that the sinless Christ was made sin (by imputation) with our sins, in order that in Christ we might become righteous (by imputation) with His righteousness. In consequence Christ has no sin but ours, and we have no righteousness but His. *John Stott*

SO WHAT?

The truths about imputation reveal why the Gospel is such good news—why we can and should praise the God of our salvation.

Adoption

IN TEN WORDS OR LESS

God makes believers His children, and they become His heirs.

DETAILS, PLEASE

Only the apostle Paul uses the word *adoption* in scripture. This family-related action involves the rights and responsibilities of those who enter God's family by faith in Christ.

Romans 9:4 refers to Israel's national adoption, separating them from other nations and giving them special privileges. Romans 8 describes God adopting individuals in salvation who were formerly "carnally minded" and in "enmity against God" (verses 6–7). They received the Spirit of adoption to address God with intimate language, "Abba, Father" (verse 15), and are considered "children of the living God" (Romans 9:26). With this new acceptance in God's family, Jesus "is not ashamed to call them brethren" (Hebrews 2:11).

This adoption was part of God's eternal plan from the *past* (Ephesians 1:5). Romans 8:13–16 speaks of God's Spirit providing assurance of adoption in the *present*, by empowering believers to overcome deeds of the flesh. This adoption includes becoming God's heirs anticipating a glorious *future* inheritance, including "the redemption of our body" (Romans 8:23) enhancing Christian hope (1 John 3:2–3).

ADDITIONAL SCRIPTURES

- And [I] will be a Father unto you, and ye shall be my sons and daughters, saith the Lord Almighty. (2 Corinthians 6:18)
- But when the fullness of time had come, God sent forth his Son, born of woman, born under the law, to redeem those who were under the law, so that we might receive adoption as sons. (Galatians 4:4–5 ESV)

WHAT OTHERS SAY

While it costs us a lot to adopt children, it cost God the blood of His own Son. *Ricky Morton*

SO WHAT?

Knowing we are God's children gives us great confidence for life. As a loving Father, He will protect and provide for His own.

Sanctification

IN TEN WORDS OR LESS

Sanctification means God sets us apart for His special use.

DETAILS, PLEASE

Sanctification is God's work of making believers righteous by separating them from sin to become Christlike. Of three aspects, the first is *positional* sanctification. 1 Corinthians 1:2 (NKJV) mentions those "who are sanctified in Christ Jesus, called to be saints" (see also 6:11). This is being set apart once for all from sin's penalty and is the same as justification.

Next, *progressive* sanctification describes daily Christian living. Paul said, "he which hath began a good work in you will perform it until the day of Jesus Christ" (Philippians 1:6; see also 2:12–13). This describes spiritual growth and gradually being set apart from sin's power "until Christ be formed in you" (Galatians 4:19; see also 2 Corinthians 3:18).

Finally, *perfected* sanctification refers to future glorification. Then believers will be "conformed to the image of [God's] Son. . . [and] also glorified" (Romans 8:29–30).

ADDITIONAL SCRIPTURES

- And the very God of peace sanctify you wholly; and I pray God your whole spirit and soul and body be preserved blameless unto the coming of our Lord Jesus Christ. (1 Thessalonians 5:23)
- Therefore, if anyone cleanses himself from these things, he will be a vessel for honor, sanctified, useful to the Master, prepared for every good work. (2 Timothy 2:21 NASB)

WHAT OTHERS SAY

The Christian life requires hard work. Our sanctification is a process wherein we are coworkers with God. We have the promise of God's assistance in our labor, but His divine help does not annul our responsibility to work. *R. C. Sproul*

SO WHAT?

Those who hope to become like Christ upon His return purify themselves now while waiting for His appearing.

Born Again

IN TEN WORDS OR LESS

Through trusting Christ, believers receive spiritual life from God.

DETAILS, PLEASE

Being born again involves an instantaneous change from spiritual death to spiritual life (John 5:24). Jesus clarified this to Nicodemus (John 3:1–21), speaking of the necessity of the new birth to "see" (verse 3) or "enter" (verse 5) God's kingdom.

A person must be "born of water and of the Spirit" (verse 5), best understood as spiritual water and renewal, predicted in Ezekiel 36:24–27. Jesus then compared this to the power of the invisible wind (John 3:8), and to Moses placing a bronze serpent on a pole to save people bitten by poisonous snakes (John 3:14; see also Numbers 21:1–9). Finally, it's like coming out of darkness into light (John 3:19–21).

Was Nicodemus ever born again? His involvement in Jesus' burial is evidence that he became a believer (John 19:38–42).

ADDITIONAL SCRIPTURES

- Blessed be the God and Father of our Lord Jesus Christ, who according to His great mercy has caused us to be born again to a living hope through the resurrection of Jesus Christ from the dead. (1 Peter 1:3 NASB)

- For you have been born again, not of perishable seed, but of imperishable, through the living and enduring word of God. (1 Peter 1:23 NIV)

WHAT OTHERS SAY

The point that Jesus wanted to hammer home to Nicodemus is. . . "You need to be born again! You need to see yourself as a sinner who needs more than moral and religious improvement. You need nothing less than new life from God!" *Steven J. Cole*

SO WHAT?

Evidence for the new birth is having a new hope in a living Savior who died for us.

Grace

Grace is God's free and unmerited blessings to undeserving people.

DETAILS, PLEASE

The apostle Paul frequently began and ended his New Testament letters by seeking God's undeserved kindness for others, saying, "Grace to you." The following shows how divine grace functions throughout the entire Christian life:

Saving grace (Ephesians 2:8–10): Paul said that God's salvation is received as a gift by grace through faith and is not earned by a person's good works (verses 8–9). Those who are saved then produce good works (verse 10). In Romans 11:5–6 Paul clarified that grace and works both have their place but cannot be mixed; otherwise grace is no longer true grace.

Sustaining grace (2 Corinthians 12:7–10): Paul learned about God's gracious power not just to heal, but also to assist him during chronic personal suffering while waiting for relief from his "thorn in the flesh." The Lord told him, "My grace is sufficient for you" (verse 9 NKJV). In 2 Timothy 2:1 Paul spoke about this from his experience of end-of-life suffering from persecution, instructing Timothy to be "strong in the grace that is in Christ Jesus." The apostle Peter gave this exhortation in 1 Peter 5:12 (ESV): "This is the true grace of God. Stand firm in it."

Sanctifying grace (Titus 2:11–14): Paul said that the "grace of God that brings salvation has appeared to all men, teaching us" (verses 11–12 NKJV). What he taught was that Jesus' message is for everyone, and those He saves He changes to become holy. The stated purpose of Christ's death is to redeem and purify us (verse 14).

Serving grace (Romans 12:6): This refers to God empowering and directing believers to serve Him. Paul's own testimony was "By the grace of God I am what I am" (1 Corinthians 15:10). Paul, the persecutor, became a preacher who served God abundantly. In 1 Peter 4:10, Peter spoke about believers as stewards effectively managing spiritual gifts ("manifold grace") that God entrusts to each one.

Sharing grace (2 Corinthians 9:7–8): God teaches believers to give as He gives, joyfully sharing personal possessions with others in need. The words "God is able to make all grace abound toward you" (verse 8) speaks of God supplying material possessions to gladly share with others because "God loveth a cheerful giver" (verse 7).

The New Testament ends with this benediction: "The grace of our Lord Jesus Christ be with you all. Amen" (Revelation 22:21).

ADDITIONAL SCRIPTURES

- But he giveth more grace. Wherefore he saith, God resisteth the proud, but giveth grace unto the humble. (James 4:6)
- Let us then approach God's throne of grace with confidence, so that we may receive mercy and find grace to help us in our time of need. (Hebrews 4:16 NIV)

WHAT OTHERS SAY

Ascribed to God, grace is His voluntary, unrestrained, unmerited favor toward guilty sinners, granting them justification and life instead of the penalty of death, which they deserved. *Herman Bavinck*

SO WHAT?

As God's "beloved," believers should be careful not to fall from steadfastness, but to grow in grace and knowledge of our Lord and Savior, Jesus Christ.

Faith

Faith is a confident hope in the truths of God.

DETAILS, PLEASE

Faith is defined as the "confidence in what we hope for and assurance about what we do not see" (Hebrews 11:1 NIV). This is not blind faith. The foundation of the Christian faith is the inspired and inerrant word of God in scripture (Psalm 19:7–11; 2 Timothy 3:16), which speaks of His trustworthy nature and providence (Psalm 37:5–6; Romans 8:28).

Abraham possessed this type of faith. His reputation was this: he was "fully convinced that what [God] had promised He was also able to perform" (Romans 4:21 NKJV). After waiting for twenty-five years after God promised Him a child, his wife Sarah "bore Abraham a son in his old age" (Genesis 21:2 NKJV).

The author of Hebrews devoted all of chapter 11 to this theme and noted, "Without faith it is impossible to please [God]" (verse 6 NKJV). Faith that pleases Him involves two things. First, we "must believe that He is," meaning we trust what He has revealed about Himself. And second, that He is benevolent, "a rewarder of those who diligently seek Him" (verse 6 NKJV).

ADDITIONAL SCRIPTURES

- For the scripture says, "Whoever believes in Him will not be disappointed." (Romans 10:11 NASB)
- Believe in the LORD your God, so shall ye be established; believe his prophets, so shall ye prosper. (2 Chronicles 20:20)

WHAT OTHERS SAY

Faith is a refusal to panic. *Martyn Lloyd-Jones*

SO WHAT?

Faith means we have confidence in God as He is described in the scriptures and trust in Him through the power of the Holy Spirit.

Repentance

IN TEN WORDS OR LESS
Repentance is contrition resulting in change of heart and life.

DETAILS, PLEASE
Repentance is described in 1 Thessalonians 1:9 (NKJV): "You turned to God from idols to serve the living and true God." These believers changed their minds about idolatry and displayed saving faith in Christ. Regarding sorrow for sin, in 2 Corinthians 7:9–10 (NKJV), the apostle Paul described a difference between "the sorrow of the world," resulting in death, and "godly sorrow [producing] repentance leading to salvation. This difference is seen between Peter, who experienced genuine repentance about denying the Lord and was restored (Luke 22:32–33, 60–62; John 21:15–19), and Judas, who only had hopeless regret for betraying the Lord and committed suicide (Matthew 27:3–5).

Luke adds this about repentance in Acts: It is given by God for forgiveness of sins (5:31; 11:18); it is seen in God's gracious command (17:29–31); it accompanies faith in Christ (20:21); and it produces appropriate works as evidence of its presence (26:20).

ADDITIONAL SCRIPTURES
- Therefore I will judge you, O house of Israel, every one according to his ways, saith the Lord GOD. Repent, and turn yourselves from all your transgressions; so iniquity shall not be your ruin. (Ezekiel 18:30)
- "I say to you that likewise there will be more joy in heaven over one sinner who repents then over ninety-nine just persons who need no repentance." (Luke 15:7 NKJV)

WHAT OTHERS SAY
Repentance is more than simply being sorry for sin. It is agreeing with God that you are sinful, confessing your sins to Him, and making a conscious choice to turn from sin and pursue holiness (Isaiah 55:7). *John MacArthur*

SO WHAT?
We should practice repentance and live with a repentant spirit until we arrive in glory, when these things become obsolete.

Forgiveness

IN TEN WORDS OR LESS

Forgiveness is God's merciful pardon for sins committed.

DETAILS, PLEASE

Forgiveness is an expression of God's loving-kindness that we can enjoy. Moses knew this when he sought God's forgiveness for Israel's great sin in the golden calf incident (Exodus 32:30–32). God gave this declaration about Himself: "The LORD, the LORD God, merciful and gracious, longsuffering, and abundant in goodness and truth, keeping mercy for thousands, forgiving iniquity, and transgression and sin" (Exodus 34:6–7).

Israel's prophets provided memorable pictures of divine pardon. Isaiah gave several images: "Though your sins be as scarlet, they shall be as white as snow" (Isaiah 1:18); God has "cast all [our] sins behind [his] back" as one disposing of something worthless (Isaiah 38:17); He "blots out [our] transgressions" and says "I will not remember your sins" (Isaiah 43:25 NKJV). He stated, "I have swept away your offenses like a cloud, your sins like the morning mist" (Isaiah 44:22 NIV). The prophet Micah offered these two pictures: "[God] will tread our sins underfoot and hurl all our iniquities into the depths of the sea" (Micah 7:19 NIV). King David, also called a prophet, stated, "As far as the east is from the west, so far has he removed our transgressions from us" (Psalm 103:12 NIV).

In the New Testament, Paul took his readers to Calvary's cross, highlighting the scene of Jesus' sacrificial death that removes the guilt of our sins and makes all Old Testament pictures meaningful. Jesus, Paul said, "canceled out the certificate of debt consisting of decrees against us, which was hostile to us; and He has taken it out of the way, having nailed it to the cross" (Colossians 2:14 NASB).

The apostle Peter spoke about a once-for-all judicial forgiveness from God as our Judge that's needed to *enter* His family. "Through His name [Jesus Christ] everyone who believes in Him receives forgiveness of sins" (Acts 10:42–43 NASB; see also 13:38–39). John also referred to parental forgiveness from God as our heavenly Father, for those already *in* His family: "If we confess our sins, He is faithful and just to forgive us our sins and to cleanse us from all unrighteousness" (1 John 1:9 NKJV). Here the word *confess* means "to say the same thing" as God does about our sins, indicating our agreement with Him and our genuine repentance for our sins. As Proverbs 28:13 (NIV) says, "Whoever conceals their sins does not prosper, but the one who confesses and renounces them finds mercy."

Believers have a practical responsibility toward one another, when it's needed, to display kindness with a tender heart to forgive one another, "even as God in Christ forgave you" (Ephesians 4:32 NKJV). This attitude and action involve our trust in the work of the Holy Spirit of God to assist us (verse 30).

ADDITIONAL SCRIPTURES

- "And forgive us our debts, as we forgive our debtors." (Matthew 6:12 NKJV)
- For if ye forgive men their trespasses, your heavenly Father will also forgive you: but if ye forgive not men their trespasses, neither will your Father forgive your trespasses. (Matthew 6:14–15)

WHAT OTHERS SAY

Sins are so remitted, as if they never were committed. *Thomas Adams*

SO WHAT?

Those who have been forgiven by God should stand in awe of Him—and forgive others for their offenses.

Righteousness

IN TEN WORDS OR LESS

Righteousness is the quality of conforming to God's law.

DETAILS, PLEASE

Righteousness is a major theme in the book of Romans, which reveals its various aspects. It first denotes the character of God, who is perfectly righteous (3:5, 24–26). Second, Romans reveals mankind as unrighteous, as sinners: "There is none righteous, no, not one" (Romans 3:10; see also verse 23). This negates the human tendency to evaluate ourselves with an instinctive self-righteousness that God rejects. Third, sinners are made righteous through faith in Christ's work (3:21–22). God in His grace gives righteousness as a gift to believers, making them acceptable to Him (Romans 5:17–18; 10:3, 10; see also Isaiah 45:8). Finally, Christians are to pursue practical righteousness in daily living because of their new status with God by using the scriptures for direction (Romans 6:13, 16–19; 14:17–19; see also 2 Timothy 2:22).

In the future, when He judges the world, the righteous Judge will give crowns of righteousness as rewards (Acts 17:31; 2 Timothy 4:8).

ADDITIONAL SCRIPTURES

- Blessed are they which do hunger and thirst after righteousness: for they shall be filled. (Matthew 5:6)
- Awake to righteousness, and sin not; for some have not the knowledge of God: I speak this to your shame. (1 Corinthians 15:34)

WHAT OTHERS SAY

The wisdom of God devised a way for the love of God to deliver sinners from the wrath of God while not compromising the righteousness of God. *John Piper*

SO WHAT?

God calls us to walk in His right ways (or righteousness) and shows us how to do that.

Liberty

Jesus Christ offers true freedom to everyone enslaved to sin.

DETAILS, PLEASE

As Jesus began His public ministry, during a synagogue service He read a messianic prophecy that included these words: "He hath anointed me. . .to preach deliverance to the captives. . .to set at liberty them that are bruised" (Luke 4:18). Throughout His entire ministry, Jesus found it necessary to correct false expectations about a Messiah whom Israel believed would provide national and political liberation from the Roman Empire. During Jesus' first advent, His message was primarily about a spiritual kingdom where spiritual freedom from sin and death could be found. At His trial He explained to Pilate, "My kingdom is not of this world" (John 18:36). The kind of freedom that He preached was personal and spiritual, a freedom from the awful effects of sin (John 8:34). This liberty was found in Him. He said, "Ye shall know the truth, and the truth shall make you free" (John 8:32), and "If the Son therefore shall make you free, ye shall be free indeed" (verse 36).

The apostle Paul described the Christian's "emancipation proclamation." He said in Galatians 3:13 (NKJV), "Christ has redeemed us from the curse of the law, having become a curse for us." In Romans 6 he explained two kinds of spiritual slavery. Unbelievers are described as "slaves. . .of sin leading to death" (verse 16 NKJV). But Paul also said that believers, united with Christ in His death and resurrection, are delivered and empowered to live for Him (verse 4) since they have been freed from the second kind of slavery, sin's domination and power (verse 7). He thanked God for those who believed the Gospel and responded in obedient faith. They had "been set free from sin" and had become "slaves of righteousness" (verse 18 NKJV).

When questions surfaced about "gray areas" in Christian liberty, Paul gave this advice: Always glorify God in whatever you do (1 Corinthians 10:31). Never become a stumbling block that hinders others (Romans 14:13). Walk in brotherly love (Romans 14:15). Seek peace and build up others (Romans 14:19).

ADDITIONAL SCRIPTURES

- For though I am free from all men, I have made myself a slave to all, so that I may win more. (1 Corinthians 9:19 NASB)

- It is for freedom that Christ has set us free. Stand firm, then, and do not let yourselves be burdened again by a yoke of slavery. (Galatians 5:1 NIV)

- Live as free people, but do not use your freedom as a cover-up for evil; live as God's slaves. (1 Peter 2:16 NIV)

WHAT OTHERS SAY

God's purpose in redeeming men from sin is not to give them freedom to do as they please but freedom to do as He pleases, which is to live righteously. *John MacArthur*

SO WHAT?

Our calling to Christian freedom replaces our former bondage to self-centeredness. Our new concern should be how to best serve each other through love.

Humility

IN TEN WORDS OR LESS
Humility is having a modest opinion about our importance.

DETAILS, PLEASE
Paul spoke about humility in Philippians 2, attempting to solve the highly contagious problem of conflict among believers. He first urged the development of Spirit-filled humility in our opinion about ourselves, to promote and protect love, joy, and unity with others (verses 1–4). Arguing and self-promotion must be replaced with humility toward others, as we view them and their concerns as more important than ourselves. To encourage this thinking, Paul cited the powerful example of "Christ Jesus" who thought and acted this way (verses 5–8). His was unmatched condescension since He existed in heavenly glory "in the form of God" (verse 6). Becoming incarnate, He lived among men as an inconspicuous servant. In humble obedience to God's will, He accomplished His mission to die for our sins as a criminal on the cross. His honor was that "God. . . has highly exalted Him" (verse 9 NKJV).

ADDITIONAL SCRIPTURES
- Humble yourselves in the sight of the Lord, and he shall lift you up. (James 4:10)
- Likewise you younger people, submit yourselves to your elders. Yes, all of you be submissive to one another, and be clothed with humility, for "God resists the proud, but gives grace to the humble." (1 Peter 5:5 NKJV)

WHAT OTHERS SAY
Growth in grace is growth downward; it is the forming of a lower estimate of ourselves; it is a deepening realization of our nothingness; it is a heartfelt recognition that we are not worthy of the least of God's mercies. *Arthur W. Pink*

SO WHAT?
The prophet Micah rhetorically asked what God requires from His people. His threefold answer was "to do justly, and to love mercy, and to *walk humbly* with thy God" (6:8, emphasis added).

Chastisement

IN TEN WORDS OR LESS
God wisely disciplines us so we become holy like Him.

DETAILS, PLEASE
Hebrews 12 gives a memorable "word of encouragement" (verse 5 NIV) for God's children by quoting Proverbs 3:11–12, exhorting believers not to resent the Lord's discipline, since He effectively uses hardship. A false notion needed correction, namely, that trouble in our lives means that God doesn't love us! First, difficulties represent evidence of the Lord's love (verses 6–8). Good parents correct their children. To be without problems might indicate that a person is not a believer.

Next, in verses 9–10 a comparison is made, reasoning from the lesser to the greater. Children learned to give reverence to an earthly father, after receiving flawed correction. So believers who now receive perfect discipline should give humble reverence to the "Father of spirits" who only seeks His children's well-being and holiness (verse 9 NIV).

Verse 11 states the conclusion that the pain associated with chastisement is never pleasant, but for those interested in maturing, "a harvest of righteousness and peace" (NIV) can be produced.

ADDITIONAL SCRIPTURES
* Blessed is the man whom You chasten, O LORD, and whom You teach out of Your law. (Psalm 94:12 NASB)
* As many as I love, I rebuke and chasten; be zealous therefore, and repent. (Revelation 3:19)

WHAT OTHERS SAY
The man who accepts discipline at the hand of God as something designed by his heavenly Father for his good will ceases to feel resentful and rebellious. *F. F. Bruce*

SO WHAT?
A good prayer to our Father can be, "It is good for me that I have been afflicted, that I might learn thy statutes" (Psalm 119:71).

Hope

IN TEN WORDS OR LESS

Biblical hope is based on the reliability of God's promises.

DETAILS, PLEASE

The apostle Paul shared a prayerful wish for Christians in Romans 15:13, saying that true hope is found in "the God of hope" who fills the lives of believers "with all joy and peace in believing, that [they] may abound in hope, through the power of the Holy Ghost." These are encouraging words for people who have only known uncertainties and disappointments (1 Corinthians 15:19) or have "no hope" and are "without God in the world" (Ephesians 2:12).

Biblical hope is not wishful thinking built on sinking sand, but trust in the person of Jesus Christ (1 Timothy 1:1), who faithfully keeps His word. Abraham testified of God's ability to keep His promises, believing that "what He had promised He was also able to perform" (Romans 4:21 NKJV). Joshua's testimony at the end of his life was "not one thing has failed of all the good things which the LORD your God spoke" (Joshua 23:14 NKJV).

Others helped to describe different aspects of this hope. One picture is given of this hope as "an anchor of the soul," attached to God's most holy presence, where Jesus our forerunner has already gone, indicating that His promises are unchangeable (Hebrews 6:17–20 NKJV). Suffering saints found comfort in the witness of Jeremiah, who discovered renewed hope during national tragedy, through meditating on God's great faithfulness (Lamentations 3:18–26). Peter, who in church history was called "the apostle of hope," said that believers have been "born again to a living hope through the resurrection of Jesus Christ from the dead" (1 Peter 1:3 NASB). This hope is alive because it's rooted in Christ, who once was dead and is alive forevermore, giving new life to believers. Paul also connected this hope to eternal life (Titus 3:7) and said that "we were saved in this hope" (Romans 8:24 NKJV).

It was God's grace that taught Paul to look toward the future for Christ's glorious appearing, which he called "the blessed hope" (Titus 2:13 NKJV). The apostle John described Christ's return as a purifying hope that motivates believers to rid their lives of sin, since they realize that one day they will be like Him (1 John 3:2–3).

ADDITIONAL SCRIPTURES

- Blessed are those whose help is the God of Jacob, whose hope is in the LORD their God. (Psalm 146:5 NIV)
- We have fixed our hope on the living God, who is the Savior of all men, especially of believers. (1 Timothy 4:10 NASB)
- For whatsoever things were written aforetime were written for our learning, that we through patience and comfort of the scriptures might have hope. (Romans 15:4)

WHAT OTHERS SAY

Optimism is a wish without warrant; Christian hope is a certainty, guaranteed by God himself. . . . Christian hope expresses knowledge that every day of his life, and every moment beyond it, the believer can say with truth, on the basis of God's own commitment, that the best is yet to come. *J. I. Packer*

SO WHAT?

Everyone should hear about this hope! So believers should be hopeful people ready to give others respectful biblical answers.

Church

IN TEN WORDS OR LESS

"The church" is all Christian believers, unified by God's Spirit.

DETAILS, PLEASE

The word *church* means "called out ones." The universal church includes all true believers in Christ globally (1 Corinthians 12:12–13), with new members added when they are saved (Acts 2:47). The church's great commission involves making disciples (Matthew 28:18–20). Most churches—individual bodies of the global church—observe two rituals symbolizing a believer's union to Christ's death and resurrection: water baptism (Romans 6:3–4) and Communion, also called the Lord's Table (Matthew 26:26–29).

Among illustrations that help explain it, the church is compared to a *body* (Romans 12:5) with Christ as the head (Colossians 1:18), directing every part and giving spiritual gifts (1 Corinthians 12:14–31). It is viewed as a *building* whose foundation is Jesus Christ (1 Corinthians 3:9–15), who is also the chief cornerstone (1 Peter 2:6–7). And it is described as the *bride* of Christ celebrating a heavenly marriage feast (Revelation 19:7–9).

ADDITIONAL SCRIPTURES

- He that hath an ear, let him hear what the Spirit saith unto the churches. (Revelation 3:22)
- "And I tell you, you are Peter, and on this rock I will build my church, and the gates of hell shall not prevail against it." (Matthew 16:18 ESV)

WHAT OTHERS SAY

These then are the marks of the ideal Church—love, suffering, holiness, sound doctrine, genuineness, evangelism, and humility. They are what Christ desires to find in His churches as He walks among them. *John Stott*

SO WHAT?

The church—true believers in Jesus—gather to worship on the Lord, feed on His Word, and edify one another.

Pastor

IN TEN WORDS OR LESS

A church leader called by God to shepherd a congregation.

DETAILS, PLEASE

Paul the apostle describes pastors as being given by God (Ephesians 4:11). They're also known by other titles, including elders, shepherds, overseers, and bishops (1 Peter 5:1–2; Acts 20:28; 1 Timothy 3:2).

Because of their holy calling and the dangers of wolves in sheeps' clothing, pastors are to meet numerous qualifications. Listed in 1 Timothy 3:1–7, they include a personal conviction for this "good work" (verse 1), an exemplary family life, good moral and social qualities, and a sensitivity to the devil's efforts to destroy a Christian's testimony among unbelievers (verses 2–7). They're to be acknowledged as persons devoted to the study and teaching of the scriptures (1 Timothy 5:17–18). A similar list appears in Titus 1:5–9. In Hebrews 13, God described the way pastors should be treated by their congregations. They're to be remembered (verse 7), to receive cooperative obedience since "they watch for your souls" (verse 17), and to receive friendly greetings (verse 24).

ADDITIONAL SCRIPTURES

- But we request of you, brethren, that you appreciate those who diligently labor among you, and have charge over you in the Lord and give you instruction, and that you esteem them very highly in love because of their work. Live in peace with one another. (1 Thessalonians 5:12–13 NASB)

WHAT OTHERS SAY

The great design and intention of the office of a Christian preacher [is] to restore the throne and dominion of God in the souls of men ...into a state of everlasting friendship with him. *Cotton Mather*

SO WHAT?

Church members should be thankful for pastors who love Jesus and feed His sheep.

Missionary

A missionary takes the Gospel message to the lost.

DETAILS, PLEASE

This word is not found in scripture, but it's used today to describe those who spread the Gospel. Scripture certainly addresses missionary work. Before Jesus ascended, He told His followers (in Acts 1:8) that they would be indwelt by the Holy Spirit to become His witnesses. Their work would begin in Jerusalem and expand from there to "the uttermost part of the earth." The book of Matthew ends with Jesus' command called the Great Commission (Matthew 28:18–20). In it He announced His universal authority for this work done in His name (verse 18). He then commanded that disciples (devoted followers) be made among all nations by believers who are going, baptizing, and teaching (verse 19). And He promised His encouraging presence with them (verse 20). Those effective in this work are gifted as "evangelists" (Ephesians 4:11). Paul's protégé Timothy was encouraged to do this work (2 Timothy 4:2–5).

ADDITIONAL SCRIPTURES

- Sing to the LORD, bless His name; proclaim good tidings of His salvation from day to day. Tell of His glory among the nations, His wonderful deeds among all the peoples. (Psalm 96:2–3 NASB)

- The harvest truly is great, but the labourers are few: pray ye therefore the Lord of the harvest, that he would send forth labourers into his harvest. (Luke 10:2)

WHAT OTHERS SAY

I almost wish I had a hundred bodies; they should all be devoted to my Savior in the missionary cause. *Hudson Taylor*

SO WHAT?

It's been said that a person is either a missionary or a mission field. Which are you?

Baptism

IN TEN WORDS OR LESS

Water ritual pictures believers' identification with Christ's death and resurrection.

DETAILS, PLEASE

John the Baptist preached a "baptism of repentance for the remission of sins" (Mark 1:4). He baptized repentant people who confessed their sins. Jesus, who had no sin, surprised everyone when *He* asked to be baptized. He explained His need "to fulfil all righteousness" (Matthew 3:15). In doing this, Jesus identified with all sinners as their example and anticipated His own baptism of suffering death (Matthew 20:22). During an intentional transition from John to Jesus, people would be baptized once in Jesus' name (John 3:22, 26, 30; 4:1–2). This became the norm, since the Messiah had arrived to die and rise again (Acts 2:38; 8:12, 35–38). The repeated pattern in Acts was for people to believe and then be baptized (Acts 2:41; 8:36–38; 9:17–18; 10:44–48; 16:30–33).

ADDITIONAL SCRIPTURES

- But when they believed Philip preaching the things concerning the kingdom of God, and the name of Jesus Christ, they were baptized, both men and women. (Acts 8:12)
- For by one Spirit are we all baptized into one body, whether we be Jews or Gentiles, whether we be bond or free; and have been all made to drink into one Spirit. (1 Corinthians 12:13)

WHAT OTHERS SAY

Water baptism was extremely important in the early church, not as a means of salvation or special blessing but as a testimony of identity with and unity in Jesus Christ. *John MacArthur*

SO WHAT?

Those being baptized should understand its meaning so that they can confidently and joyfully give their personal testimony.

Communion

IN TEN WORDS OR LESS

This ritual for believers involves remembering the Lord's death.

DETAILS, PLEASE

The Lord's instructions for this ritual originated at the Last Supper, when He gave His disciples new meaning to their Passover observance, which now pointed to the death of the Lamb of God (1 Corinthians 11:23–32). This ceremony of thanksgiving remembers Jesus' substitutionary suffering and death. Eating bread represents Jesus' broken body, and drinking the "fruit of the vine" (Matthew 26:29) represents His atoning shed blood. This memorial service was a visual proclamation of trust, looking back to Jesus' death and looking forward to His return.

To honor the Lord, participants were warned about participating in an unworthy manner, and commanded to "examine" themselves (1 Corinthians 11:28). Some of the Corinthian Christians were found guilty and physically "chastened of the Lord" (verse 32).

ADDITIONAL SCRIPTURES

- The cup of blessing which we bless, is it not the communion of the blood of Christ? The bread which we break, is it not the communion of the body of Christ? (1 Corinthians 10:16)
- Verily I say unto you, I will drink no more of the fruit of the vine, until that day that I drink it new in the kingdom of God. (Mark 14:25)

WHAT OTHERS SAY

In coming to [the Communion] service the believer comes to meet with Christ and have fellowship with Him at His invitation. The examination takes place because it would be hypocrisy for us to pretend that we are in communion with the Holy One while actually cherishing known sin in our hearts. *James Montgomery Boice*

SO WHAT?

We should experience many emotions—sorrow for sins, reverence and gratitude for the Lord's death and forgiveness, and gladness about His return—when we experience Communion.

Discipleship

A training program to learn Christian doctrine, lifestyle, and service.

DETAILS, PLEASE

As Jesus ended His earthly ministry, He gave instructions about discipleship in Matthew 28:18–20. The Lord announced His authority over all things in verse 18, speaking about the activities of the mission, which are built on His authority. His main command was "make disciples of all nations" (NIV), which involves more than just conversion. A disciple is a follower, a learner, an apprentice. The global mission field includes all nationalities and people groups, rather than just Israel. The task involves three steps: (1) *going* everywhere to evangelize new followers, (2) *baptizing* in water in the name of the one triune God ("the Father, the Son, and the Holy Spirit") as a public display of genuine faith, and (3) *teaching* obedience to all of His commands so that believers become "doers of the word" (James 1:22). Initial conversion is followed by personal maturing and outreach; for encouragement Jesus promised His spiritual presence to empower His disciples (Matthew 28:19–20).

Years later, as a Roman prisoner anticipating his imminent death, the apostle Paul gave Timothy, his son in the faith, important final advice about discipleship from his years of experience (2 Timothy 2:1–7 NIV). He began by talking about needed spiritual power for this work by being "strong in the grace that is in Christ Jesus" (verse 1). He then said that the truth taught to Timothy must be passed along, a command that includes four emphases. First, "things *you* [young Timothy] have heard *me* say." These were "heard in the presence of *many witnesses*" and "entrust[ed] to *reliable people*." Finally, it was to be shared with those "qualified to teach *others*" (emphasis added). This describes a reproduction and multiplication process.

To show the seriousness of this work, Paul used three illustrations. First, it involves enduring hardship in battle "like a good soldier of Jesus Christ," whose aim is pleasing his commander who chose him for his mission, and by not being "entangled in civilian affairs" (verses 3–4 NIV). It is also like an athlete who wins competitions playing by the rules, doing God's work in God's way (verse 5 NIV). Finally, it's like "the hardworking farmer" who receives the rewards of the harvest (verse 6 NIV). The Lord gives insight and conviction about these matters (verse 7).

ADDITIONAL SCRIPTURES

- But you must continue in the things which you have learned and been assured of, knowing from whom you have learned them. (2 Timothy 3:14 NKJV)

- By this shall all men know that ye are my disciples, if ye have love one to another. (John 13:35)

- Older women. . .are to teach what is good, and so train the young women to love their husbands and children, to be self-controlled, pure, working at home, kind, and submissive to their own husbands, that the word of God may not be reviled. (Titus 2:3–5 ESV)

WHAT OTHERS SAY

A disciple is literally a follower, a pupil, a learner, an apprentice. He is one who has decided not only to follow his master but also to become like Him. *Dann Spader and Gary Mayes*

SO WHAT?

We should be growing in God's truth ourselves and looking for others to share it with.

Prayer

IN TEN WORDS OR LESS

Praying is the way we communicate with God.

DETAILS, PLEASE

Prayer connects us with our Lord as we honestly communicate with Him. In His Sermon on the Mount, Jesus spoke about two important prayer problems. One was hypocritical public praying that should be replaced with sincere private praying (Matthew 6:5–6). The second was vain repetitions in lengthy prayers that should be amended by a realization that God knows our needs (verses 7–8).

Jesus gave a model prayer we call "the Lord's Prayer" that provides helpful guidelines. Prayer should begin with *adoration*—requesting that our Father's name be revered, for His kingdom to come to earth, and for His will to be done among us (Matthew 6:9–10). It then moves to *supplication*—requests about our physical needs for daily food (verse 11). Then it continues to *confession*—our spiritual needs of forgiveness for our sins and *protection* from the devil (verses 12–13). Some later Greek manuscripts end the prayer in verse 13 with a doxology, an expression of praise to God.

ADDITIONAL SCRIPTURES

- The effective prayer of a righteous man can accomplish much. (James 5:16 NASB)
- Do not be anxious about anything, but in every situation, by prayer and petition, with thanksgiving, present your requests to God. (Philippians 4:6 NIV)

WHAT OTHERS SAY

Prayer is the key that unlocks all the storehouses of God's infinite grace and power. *R. A. Torrey*

SO WHAT?

To encourage our prayers, God reminds us in Ephesians 3:20 (NASB) that He is the One who "is able to do far more abundantly beyond all that we ask or think, according to the power that works within us."

Confession

IN TEN WORDS OR LESS

Confession is the humble admission of sins committed against God.

DETAILS, PLEASE

Scripture records the confessions of different people who said, "I have sinned." The Lord who knows hearts looks beyond words to see if confessions are acceptable through genuine repentance or unacceptable due to bad motives.

In 2 Corinthians 7:10 (NIV) the apostle Paul described two types of sorrow for sin that produce different outcomes. "Godly sorrow brings repentance that leads to salvation and leaves no regret, but worldly sorrow brings death."

But in the following list of five confessions using the words "I have sinned," something is missing. When *Pharaoh* refused to free Israel, he spoke these words to Moses only because he was pressured by God's supernatural judgment. His repeated defiance indicated that he only wanted relief from the plagues (see Exodus 9:27; 10:16–17). *Balaam* was a false prophet who loved money so much that despite his confession he persisted in opposing God's will by selling his prophetic services (see Numbers 22:34; 2 Peter 2:15–16). As Israel entered the Promised Land, the people were commanded not to loot valuables for themselves at Jericho. *Achan* violated this directive by stealing and concealing items. His confession was forced after His crime was uncovered through an intense criminal investigation (see Joshua 7:19–25). *Saul*, Israel's first king, lacked true humility in his confession by trying to secure personal honor from the prophet Samuel (1 Samuel 15:24, 30). Finally, though Jesus' betrayer *Judas Iscariot* sometimes receives unwarranted sympathy, a closer look at all the evidence surrounding his confession reveals his insincerity (Matthew 27:4–5). Even at His last supper and arrest, Jesus gave Judas final opportunities to come clean, but he refused (Matthew 26:20–25).

Some confessions, though, carry a real understanding of sin. King David, "the man after God's own heart," made deep-rooted confessions worth imitating. Examples of his "penitential" psalms are 6, 32, 38, and 143. His most notable confession is in Psalm

51, where the beginning inscription tells us Nathan the prophet had confronted his king about his hidden sin with Bathsheba, a tragic story recorded in 2 Samuel 11–12. David's confession begins by appealing to God's mercy and loving-kindness (Psalm 51:1). Then, as he sought pardon, he thoughtfully described his crimes as "transgressions" (crossing over boundaries), "iniquity" (twisting truth), and "sin" (missing the mark, verses 2–3). He mentioned his haunting guilt, saying, "my sin is ever before me" (verse 3). David acknowledged his ultimate accountability to God and submission to His chastisement (verse 4). He concluded by seeking his own restoration and hoping that others who read his psalms might learn from his own failures (verses 5–19).

ADDITIONAL SCRIPURE

- For thy name's sake, O LORD, pardon mine iniquity; for it is great. (Psalm 25:11)

- O my God, I am too ashamed and humiliated to lift up my face to You, my God; for our iniquities have risen higher than our heads, and our guilt has grown up to the heavens. (Ezra 9:6 NKJV)

- I confess my iniquity; I am troubled by my sin. (Psalm 38:18 NIV)

WHAT OTHERS SAY

Confession should be a daily activity for the Christian, whose entire pilgrimage is characterized by the spirit of repentance. *R. C. Sproul*

SO WHAT?

When we ask God to search our hearts and reveal our wicked ways, true confession should follow.

Intercession

IN TEN WORDS OR LESS

Intercession is praying on behalf of others.

DETAILS, PLEASE

In his letters to churches, Paul frequently spoke about prayer's importance. In 1 Thessalonians 5:17 he exhorted believers to "pray without ceasing." His prison epistle to the Ephesians contains examples of intercession: Paul informed them about his prayers for them and gave them specific intercessions for himself. He continually thanked God for their faith and love and asked God that they might grow in spiritual wisdom (Ephesians 1:15–21). He also prayed for their spiritual inner strength and growth in understanding Christ's love (3:14–19). When mentioning the believer's "full armor of God," which would help them to "stand against the devil's schemes" (6:11 NIV), Paul said that believers should "pray in the Spirit. . .for all the Lord's people" (6:18 NIV). He requested the Ephesians' prayers for himself, to continue to boldly speak the mystery of the Gospel (6:19).

ADDITIONAL SCRIPTURES

- Epaphras, who is one of you, a servant of Christ, saluteth you, always labouring fervently for you in prayers, that ye may stand perfect and complete in all the will of God. (Colossians 4:12)
- Moreover, as for me, far be it from me that I should sin against the LORD in ceasing to pray for you. (1 Samuel 12:23 NKJV)

WHAT OTHERS SAY

We never know how God will answer our prayers, but we can expect that He will get us involved in His plan for the answer. If we are true intercessors, we must be ready to take part in God's work on behalf of the people for whom we pray. *Corrie ten Boom*

SO WHAT?

It's not enough to pray for ourselves. We must remember to include others in our prayers.

Fruit

IN TEN WORDS OR LESS

Fruit is a spiritual harvest from God for His glory.

DETAILS, PLEASE

"Fruit" is used figuratively in scripture in several ways. The "fruit of the Spirit" describes nine character traits in believers' lives, produced by the Holy Spirit (Galatians 5:22–23). It also refers to different types of conduct—some leading to "death" and others to "everlasting life" (Romans 6:21–22). Jesus and Paul both used the word to describe new Christian converts (John 4:35–38; Romans 1:13–16; 16:5). *Fruit* also describes conversation—our words (Matthew 12:33–37). Finally, it is used for financial contributions benefiting poor believers (Romans 15:26–28).

In John 15 Jesus used an agricultural metaphor describing fruitfulness in believers' lives. He said, "I am the true vine, and My Father is the vinedresser" (verse 1 NKJV), indicating that spiritual life flows from Him to the branches, producing "fruit." Some branches produce "no fruit," and these falsely professing believers are removed. Fruitful branches, however, are pruned to "bear more fruit" (verse 2). Through obedience and prayer, some produce "much fruit," which glorifies God (verse 8).

ADDITIONAL SCRIPTURE

- Live a life worthy of the Lord and please him in every way: bearing fruit in every good work, growing in the knowledge of God. (Colossians 1:10 NIV)

WHAT OTHERS SAY

We must do more than say we are Jesus' disciples. We must bear fruit like we are Jesus' disciples. . . . Bearing good fruit brings God glory. When we look and act like Jesus, it shows that He is good enough to save us, valuable enough to be followed, and strong enough to change us. *Kevin DeYoung*

SO WHAT?

As laborers together with God, one plants and another waters, but "God. . .gives the increase" (1 Corinthians 3:7 NKJV). Let's do our part, whatever that is.

Giving

IN TEN WORDS OR LESS
God freely gives gifts for our benefit and His glory.

DETAILS, PLEASE
The topic of giving begins with the greatest Giver, God our Savior. In Romans 8:32 (NASB) Paul said that God "did not spare His own Son, but delivered Him over for us all." This salvation is described in as a "free gift" that includes "the gift of righteousness" (Romans 5:15, 17). In Romans 6:23 Paul said, "the gift of God is eternal life through Jesus Christ our Lord." Also, in Ephesians 2:8, he stated that this salvation is "by grace. . .through faith; and that not of yourselves; it is the gift of God." Our appropriate response is, "Thanks be to God for His indescribable gift!" (2 Corinthians 9:15 NASB). Having received such blessing from God, Christians should then be generous with others. "Blessed is he that considereth the poor," David wrote; "the LORD will deliver him in time of trouble" (Psalm 41:1). David's son Solomon later noted, "The liberal soul shall be made fat: and he that watereth shall be watered also himself" (Proverbs 11:25).

ADDITIONAL SCRIPTURES
- Give, and it shall be given unto you; good measure, pressed down, and shaken together, and running over, shall men give into your bosom. For with the same measure that ye mete withal it shall be measured to you again. (Luke 6:38)
- Charge them that are rich in this world, that they be not high-minded, nor trust in uncertain riches, but in the living God, who giveth us richly all things to enjoy. (1 Timothy 6:17)

WHAT OTHERS SAY
The act of giving is a vivid reminder that it's all about God, not about us. It's saying I am not the point. He is the point. He does not exist for me. I exist for Him. *Randy Alcorn*

SO WHAT?
As stewards of God's grace, each believer has an important role to fulfill in the body of Christ.

Eternity

IN TEN WORDS OR LESS

Eternity is infinite, unmeasurable time, both past and future.

DETAILS, PLEASE

Eternity is difficult for time-bound humans to grasp. But God, who created everything including time, is eternal. In Psalm 90:1–2 (NKJV) Moses praised Him by saying, "Lord, You have been our dwelling place in all generations. Before the mountains were brought forth, or ever You had formed the earth and the world, even from everlasting to everlasting, You are God." Every generation since Adam and Eve has known God as the all-powerful, all-wise, all-benevolent Creator who has always existed.

2 Corinthians 4 indicates that living in light of eternity is a practical truth to encourage believers. The apostle Paul testified that despite the universal problems associated with Christian living (verses 8–10), believers can experience renewed thinking about personal afflictions (verse 16). This leads to considering our present afflictions as light and momentary, working for us a promised future glory that's weightier than our troubles and eternal (verse 17). By faith believers can look beyond the present to consider an eternal glory of the future that is not yet seen (verse 18).

ADDITIONAL SCRIPTURES

- For thus says the High and Lofty One who inhabits eternity, whose name is Holy: "I dwell in the high and holy place, with him who has a contrite and humble spirit, to revive the spirit of the humble." (Isaiah 57:15 NKJV)

- "The eternal God is your refuge, and underneath are the everlasting arms." (Deuteronomy 33:27 NIV)

WHAT OTHERS SAY

Eternity to the godly is a day that has no sunset; eternity to the wicked is a night that has no sunrise. *Thomas Watson*

SO WHAT?

Believers can find encouragement from God's promise that they have a prepared place reserved in heaven, forever.

Prophecy

IN TEN WORDS OR LESS

God reveals His future plans so we can prepare.

DETAILS, PLEASE

One way God shows the trustworthiness of scripture is through the fulfillment of prophecy. This study is called eschatology.

The Lord said about Himself, "I am God and there is none like Me, declaring the end from the beginning, and from ancient times things that are not yet done, saying, 'My counsel shall stand, and I will do all My pleasure'" (Isaiah 46:9–10 NKJV). God not only predicts future events but possesses the power and authority to accomplish them.

In the New Testament, the apostles claimed that God's word could be trusted. Paul stated, "All scripture is given by inspiration of God [*breathed out by God*: ESV], and is profitable for doctrine" (2 Timothy 3:16). After referring to God's audible words, Peter spoke about God's written Word, saying "We have also a more sure word of prophecy; whereunto ye do well that ye take heed" (2 Peter 1:19).

Bible prophecy centers around Jesus Christ. The apostle John said, "The testimony of Jesus is the spirit of prophecy" (Revelation 19:10). Jesus' first disciples announced, "We have found him, of whom Moses in the law, and the prophets, did write, Jesus of Nazareth" (John 1:45). As Jesus began in ministry, He said, "Today this Scripture is fulfilled in your hearing" (Luke 4:21 NKJV). The repeated refrain in the Gospels was that things were done, "that it might be fulfilled" (Matthew 1:22; 13:34–35; 21:4; 27:35). As the time for His death and resurrection approached, Jesus reminded His followers that these things had been predicted much earlier: "Behold, we go up to Jerusalem, and *all things* that are written by the prophets concerning the Son of man shall be accomplished" (Luke 18:31, emphasis added).

As the resurrected Jesus prepared to return to heaven, He said, "I will come again" (John 14:3). The promise of the Lord's return is the great hope of believers, but He knows that unbelieving critics will mock, saying, "Where is the promise of His coming?" (2 Peter 3:4 NKJV). He responds that one of the reasons for His delayed return is because "the Lord. . .is longsuffering toward us, not willing that any should perish, but that all should come to repentance" (verse 9 NKJV).

ADDITIONAL SCRIPTURES

- Blessed is he who reads and those who hear the words of the prophecy, and heed the things which are written in it; for the time is near. (Revelation 1:3 NASB)
- The kingdoms of this world are become the kingdoms of our Lord, and of his Christ; and he shall reign for ever and ever. (Revelation 11:15)

WHAT OTHERS SAY

Understanding Bible prophecy encourages in two unique ways. First, it serves as a reminder that God controls history. . . . Second, understanding God's promises for the future provides a solid foundation to which you can anchor your hope. . . . When you reflect on God's plans and promises for you and for the world, you can face the future without fear. *John MacArthur*

SO WHAT?

The repeated warning that no one knows the time of the Lord's return (Matthew 24:36; Mark 13:32) should motivate believers to be ready.

Judgment Day

IN TEN WORDS OR LESS

Everyone will receive a final, righteous judgment from their Creator.

DETAILS, PLEASE

Since God plans to judge us, we should consider our accountability to Him. Peter said that the apostles were commanded to preach about this: "Jesus Christ, who is Lord of all. . . is the one whom God appointed as judge of the living and the dead. . . that everyone who believes in him receives forgiveness of sins" (Acts 10:36, 42–43 NIV). In Acts 17:31 Paul warned that God "appointed a day" that "he will judge the world," and "the Judge of all the earth" (Genesis 18:25) will be fair, or will judge with "righteousness" (Psalm 9:8). The appointed judge will be Jesus Christ (John 5:22, 27).

ADDITIONAL SCRIPTURES

- It is appointed unto men once to die, but after this the judgment. (Hebrews 9:27)
- You, then, why do you judge your brother or sister? . . . For we will all stand before God's judgment seat. . . . So then, each of us will give an account of ourselves to God. (Romans 14:10, 12 NIV)

WHAT OTHERS SAY

The final judgment will be done to display and glorify the righteousness of God. *Jonathan Edwards*

SO WHAT?

Every believer wants to hear the verdict, "Well done, thou good and faithful servant" (Matthew 25:21).

Resurrection

IN TEN WORDS OR LESS

Jesus' conquering of death, through resurrection, gives all Christians hope.

DETAILS, PLEASE

The Gospel message provides us with hope, especially when we're facing the fear of death. This hope is built on resurrection beliefs that began in the Old Testament. Job asked the question, "If someone dies, will they live again?" (Job 14:14 NIV). He later answered his own question, expressing hope that he and his Redeemer would "stand at the latter day upon the earth" (Job 19:25).

David penned a messianic prophecy in Psalm 16:10, referring to Christ's resurrection, which Peter (Acts 2:27) and Paul (Acts 13:36–37) both quoted in the early church age. In Daniel 12:2 the prophet spoke explicitly of end-time resurrections with different outcomes: "some to everlasting life, and some to shame and everlasting contempt."

The apostle Paul provided additional details about resurrection in 1 Corinthians 15. His Gospel message was built on Christ's atoning death and resurrection (verses 1–4). The fact that Christ rose from the dead was verified by eyewitnesses who were still alive to be consulted (verses 5–11). Paul spoke of the hopelessness of life without resurrection (verses 12–19) but referred to Christ as "the firstfruits of them that slept," indicating that future believers would also rise together to join Him (verses 20–34). They will enjoy bodies "raised in incorruption," "glory," and "power," prepared for the spiritual realm, and will "bear the image of the heavenly" (verses 35–50). These mysterious changes will produce rejoicing and thanks to God for victory over death (verses 51–57).

The resurrection truths of this chapter end in verse 58 where Paul exhorted believers to serve their risen Lord energetically, because they realize that what's done for Him is never in vain.

ADDITIONAL SCRIPTURES

- Marvel not at this: for the hour is coming, in the which all that are in the graves shall hear his voice, and shall come forth; they that have done good, unto the resurrection of life; and they that have done evil, unto the resurrection of damnation. (John 5:28–29)

- Jesus said unto her, I am the resurrection, and the life: he that believeth in me, though he were dead, yet shall he live. (John 11:25)

- And though after my skin worms destroy this body, yet in my flesh shall I see God. (Job 19:26)

WHAT OTHERS SAY

Three great, independently established facts—the empty tomb, the resurrection appearances, and the origin of the Christian faith—all point to the same marvelous conclusion: that God raised Jesus from the dead. *William Lane Craig*

SO WHAT?

Believers can offer God praise for resurrection hope by praying, "I will be satisfied when I awake with Your likeness!"

Glorification

IN TEN WORDS OR LESS

God's salvation will be completed when believers are completely remade.

DETAILS, PLEASE

This term appears in Romans 8, describing the final stage of God's salvation as He removes all sin from believers when Christ returns. Later, in Romans 13:11, Paul said, "Now is our salvation nearer than when we believed." He previously mentioned the Romans' past conversion of having been saved from sin's penalty ("justified," 5:1), and their present experience of being saved from sin's power ("sanctification," 6:22 NASB). Finally, Paul described their future of being saved from sin's presence ("glorified," 8:17–30). The J. B. Phillips New Testament gives a picturesque translation: "The whole creation is on tiptoe to see the wonderful sight of the sons of God coming into their own." This will be "magnificent liberty," being set free from sin and death (verse 21) and receiving glorified resurrected bodies (verse 23).

ADDITIONAL SCRIPTURES

- When Christ, who is our life, shall appear, then shall ye also appear with him in glory. (Colossians 3:4)
- [Christ], by the power that enables him to bring everything under his control, will transform our lowly bodies so that they will be like his glorious body. (Philippians 3:21 NIV)

WHAT OTHERS SAY

There is a day coming when all of the suffering, all of the maladies of this life are destroyed, when we, in our glorified bodies, will live in heaven, on the new earth, eternally fulfilling God's ordained purpose for us. *Paul Enns*

SO WHAT?

The purifying hope of becoming like Christ when we see Him makes us want to become more like Him now.

Second Coming

IN TEN WORDS OR LESS
Christ will gloriously return as conquering King and Judge.

DETAILS, PLEASE
Among the many prophecies about the coming Messiah were prophecies about His second coming. Sometimes Christ's two comings were combined in the same context (Isaiah 61:1–3; Luke 4:17–20). Prophecies about His first coming emphasize His suffering and death (Isaiah 53) while prophecies about His second coming describe His power, authority, and glorious rule of the earth (Isaiah 11). He confirmed that everything written about Him would be fulfilled (Luke 24:44).

When Jesus taught about His passion, He also spoke of His glorious coming, accompanied by holy angels and bestowing rewards (Matthew 16:21, 27). This would be seen and heard by all—the Son of Man coming with heavenly clouds, power, and glory, along with the sounding of trumpets (24:30–31). It would include a judgment on the nations (25:31–46).

During the Last Supper, Jesus described His return to encourage His disciples, saying He was going back to heaven, His "Father's house" with "many rooms," to prepare a special place for them (John 14:1–2 NIV). He promised to return to receive them so that they could be together forever (John 14:3; see also 1 Thessalonians 4:17). Jesus was abused by the authorities during His trials but announced that He would be honored by God when He returned (Matthew 26:64).

When the Lord ascended, two holy angels gave the disciples assurance that "this same Jesus" would "come in like manner [visibly, bodily, with clouds] as ye have seen him go into heaven" (Acts 1:11).

Christ's apostles later provided additional revelation. Paul said that Christ would return to reunite departed and living believers with the Lord (1 Thessalonians 4:13–18). He encouraged them to wait for Jesus' glorious appearing, the "blessed hope" (Titus 2:13). John gave a majestic description of the returning Christ as the conquering "King of Kings, and Lord of Lords" (Revelation 19:16). John then ended the Bible with Jesus' repeated announcement, "I come quickly" (Revelation 22:7, 12, 20), and the closing prayer we all should pray, "Even so, come Lord Jesus."

ADDITIONAL SCRIPTURES

- And Enoch also, the seventh from Adam, prophesied of these, saying, Behold, the Lord cometh with ten thousands of his saints. (Jude 14)

- Now, little children, abide in Him, so that when He appears, we may have confidence and not shrink away from Him in shame at His coming. (1 John 2:28 NASB)

- May God himself, the God of peace, sanctify you through and through. May your whole spirit, soul and body be kept blameless at the coming of our Lord Jesus Christ. (1 Thessalonians 5:23 NIV)

WHAT OTHERS SAY

The immense step from the Babe at Bethlehem to the living, reigning triumphant Lord Jesus, returning to earth for His own people—that is the glorious truth proclaimed throughout scripture. As the bells ring out the joys of Christmas, may we also be alert for the final trumpet that will announce His return, when we shall always be with Him. *Alan Redpath*

SO WHAT?

Exhortations to watchfulness and prayer surround Christ's return. All His servants must consider how they can prepare for their Lord's imminent return.

Kingdom

IN THEN WORDS OR LESS
Jesus Christ reigns as King over all His creation.

DETAILS, PLEASE
King Nebuchadnezzar of Babylon believed that he ruled over everything, until "the most High" God taught him otherwise (Daniel 4:3, 17, 25, 34–35). The nation of Israel continually hoped that their long-awaited Messiah would come to deliver them and rule the world. When John the Baptist and Jesus began preaching, people heard a new announcement: "Repent: for the kingdom of heaven is at hand" (Matthew 3:1–2; 4:17). God's kingdom was still in its mystery form as a spiritual kingdom located wherever people believed the King's message. Entrance into His kingdom requires trust in the redeeming power of Jesus Christ's blood for the forgiveness of sins (Colossians 1:12–14). Jesus assured His disciples that He will come again to earth to establish His glorious kingdom (Matthew 25:31–34).

ADDITIONAL SCRIPTURES
- The LORD has established his throne in heaven, and his kingdom rules over all. (Psalm 103:19 NIV)
- For the kingdom of God is not a matter of eating and drinking, but of righteousness, peace and joy in the Holy Spirit. (Romans 14:17 NIV)
- Fear not, little flock; for it is your Father's good pleasure to give you the kingdom. (Luke 12:32)

WHAT OTHERS SAY
The only way the kingdom of God is going to be manifest in this world before Christ comes is if we manifest it by the way we live as citizens of heaven and subjects of the King. *R. C. Sproul*

SO WHAT?
Peter encouraged believers to make sure that they "receive a rich welcome into the eternal kingdom" in heaven (2 Peter 1:11 NIV). What a joy to hear the wonderful words "Welcome home!"